VINCENZO VENEZIA

healing for daughters of emotionally absent fathers

Healing the Invisible Wounds of Childhood Emotional Neglect to Become Better Parents and Partners

ASIN: 979-12-81498-13-6

TABLE OF CONTENTS

Introduction

How are you feeling?

No, seriously, how are you *feeling*?

You might not be asked that as often as you should because your parents never had the emotional maturity to recognize that you might want to talk as well as them.

Growing up with emotionally immature parents isn't usually something we recognize until we're much older, often when we're trying to unpack our own trauma and emotions, trying not to repeat the same cycle. That's because we look up to our parents when we're children. We take their guidance and assume that they're treating us with love and wisdom, and when they provide us with everything we need—a roof over our heads, food in our bellies, and clothing—it can make it even harder to pick up on.

So, what do we do when we *do* eventually discover that our childhood wasn't exactly… normal? That our emotional needs weren't met after all?

We often identify the issue when we become more emotionally mature than our parents. Then we notice a few strange things:

- You have to care for your parents' needs as well as your own. *You* must adapt to your parents' needs; it's never the other way around.

- Your parents can't regulate their own emotions, cope with stress, or respond well to others. Mood swings seem to come from nowhere, leaving you always walking on eggshells.

- They often come across as selfish, focused far more on themselves than anyone else. If something upsets them, everyone must come to their aid immediately.

- Your parents have always been *too* involved in your life, to the point where it's controlling.

- Or the opposite is true. Your parents are passive and don't want to be involved with you and your problems. It all seems *too much* for them.

This confusing relationship where you were not treated as a child should be treated probably left you feeling insecure and very lonely. Especially when you didn't understand where these issues came from. However, understanding this can be the first step towards healing for good, especially when you discover it's often a vicious cycle.

Someone needs to break the cycle. It might not be the easiest thing in the world, but congratulations on taking the first step and working towards changing things for the future and the generations in your family to come!

But how do you heal?

I know that probably feels like an impossible task right now, but I promise you it isn't. We are creating a generation of cycle breakers. While the end goal might feel far away, if you look at each step, which this book will go into plenty of detail about to assist you along the way, these smaller steps won't be so overwhelming.

You *can* do this, and it'll be better for you when you do.

Step One: Know what's wrong.

Congratulations! By purchasing this book, you have already done that. This is a massive step in the right direction. You've not only recognized that you likely grew up with emotionally immature parents, which has had a lasting effect on you, but you also see that you want to change that. Well done! By recognizing that you want to change things for yourself and others, you're on the way.

Step Two: Work on YOU!

It's tempting to try and "fix" your parents and the issues they have faced in their lives, but unfortunately, that isn't possible. They can only change if they want to. You might know this already after suffering through terrible attempts at conversations and getting nowhere.

You have to allow them to focus on themselves while you concentrate on yourself. That will take some habit-breaking of its own. You haven't ever focused on yourself before, not fully, but now is the time. This book will help guide you through that.

Step Three: Time to Connect

You have likely spent your whole life not developing relationships properly because of the childhood you had. But before reaching out and forming a solid bond with others, you need to connect with yourself. You must dig deep and deal with shame, guilt, anger, and whatever else your parents have left you holding onto.

You might not even realize that your relationships aren't fully formed, but once you start doing the work and your relationships improve, it will become much clearer.

Step Four: Meaningful Relationships

Once you have worked on yourself and identified your destructive behavior patterns, learned productive communication skills, and established important boundaries, then you can start connecting with others.

This might not be your parents at this point, but you may wish to reach out to them at some stage. This book will also help you with that because that can be a journey on its own.

Step Five: Continue Healing

This isn't going to be just a one-time thing. You must continue your healing journey to ensure you don't slip back into old patterns. Mindfulness, therapy, and other techniques to help you live in the moment can help with this. It's a lifetime journey, but one that is totally worthwhile.

This book can assist you with *all* of this healing, giving you manageable steps, nonjudgmental advice, and different ways to heal. No one has the same experience or the same parents, and everyone responds and heals uniquely.

There is a lot of research into parental immaturity and the effect it can have on you, and for this book, I have done this for you, saving you the time of digging deep. I have read scientific studies and books and looked online, so you don't have to. Everything you need is right here, in the midst of these pages, so please, read on and gain all this knowledge for yourself.

Learning and healing from your own experiences will benefit you in ways you probably haven't even thought of yet, such as:

- Improved mental health–coping with your stress and difficult feelings will give you a much healthier mind moving forward.

- Much more happiness–emotionally mature people have greater life satisfaction and get much more joy from everything they do.

- Stronger resilience–happier people with more productive lives have a stronger mindset when dealing with problems.

The sooner you start on this healing journey, there quicker you will start feeling these benefits. Do you not want to take control of your life immediately? To take back the power that has always been taken away from you? Doesn't emotional freedom sound exciting?

You have already spent far too long under the weight of your parents and their issues. That has likely taken you away from learning who you are and what you want from your life. No more. This is *your* time. Time to be *you*.

This book will open all the right doors for you and allow you to control your healing. You can go at your own pace, making sure you don't get overwhelmed along the way.

So, why not get started and see what's in store for you? In the first chapter, we dig into what an emotionally immature parent is, so let's get started!

Part 1 - What Is an Emotionally Immature Parent?

Chapter 1: What Is an Emotionally Immature Parent?

So, how do we know that we have emotionally immature parents? That's what this first section of the book will look at. If you're unsure, or even simply want to know *how* your parents are emotionally immature, then please read on.

Emotional maturity can be thought of as an appropriate level of emotional control and expression, which makes emotional immaturity the opposite: someone who has no restraints and doesn't know how to contain themselves. Someone who is ruled by their feelings because they have never worked out how to control and express themself properly.

This means emotionally immature people often react like a child to things in an over-the-top manner. Attention-seeking behavior, name-calling, lack of communication, and avoidance behaviors are often seen in these sorts of people, making adult realities, such as parenting, very challenging.

An emotionally immature parent might appear like they simply cannot connect with other people, especially their child, but it runs much deeper than that. These people actually *fear* emotional connection and push people away, especially those closest to them.

There are many features that you're likely to pick up on once you realize that your parents are emotionally unavailable, factors that might have always been there:

- Single-mindedness and the refusal to listen to other people.

- They have no tolerance for stress or problems and can't handle feelings, so they will shut down if presented with them. They can even come across as killjoys because they dismiss other people along the way.

- Blaming others because they can't take responsibility for their own actions.

- No respect or empathy for others because they are selfish and egocentric.

- Their emotions are shallow but rapid and dramatic. Everyone is expected to cater to *their* needs, but they're only interested in the physical needs of their children.

Emotionally immature people often seem very complex on the surface but actually follow recognizable interpersonal styles, which leaves the victims and people living with them struggling with some of the following issues:

- *Isolation:* Being parented by emotionally immature people fosters a lot of loneliness. You might have grown up surrounded by people, but that didn't make you feel any less alone. They can often deal with problems that need practical solutions, but anything emotional causes them to become awkward.

- *Frustration:* Interactions with someone who doesn't have emotional maturity can feel one-sided. That's because any conversation with this person is *always* centered around them.

- *Feeling Second Best:* Guilt, shame, and fear often come with parents who flare up in blame and anger at any given moment. Your emotions become much less important, often putting you in survival mode.

- *Being Trapped:* The sense that you can't escape this situation because it's been created by the people who are supposed to love and care for you can often be anxiety-inducing.

- *Misunderstanding:* Despite being very reactive, emotionally immature parents avoid deeper feelings for fear of exposure. This often means deeper feelings aren't expressed through words, but they instead bring others to the same level of emotion as them.

- *Disrespected:* Boundaries can be really hard to set in place with emotionally immature parents. Boundaries equal rejection to them. This can lead them to being problematic and often nasty just to keep themselves on top.

- *Emotionally Drained:* Doing all the emotional work by keeping things pleasant and always being the one to say sorry can leave you feeling tired and completely worn out from the whole relationship. Not great when it's the person you have to grow up with.

- *Lost:* Being brought up by an emotionally immature parent leaves you without any autonomy over what you do with yourself. You become more of an extension of that person rather than an individual in their own right.

If any of these statements resonate with you, please continue reading because not only will you discover that you're very much not alone, but this doesn't need to be how your life continues. These cycles aren't easy to break, but you can do it.

You *can* make a difference in your own life and make things better. This book will give you the chance to take power back.

Anyone who has grown up with an emotionally immature parent is bound to be under a whole lot of pressure because of this family dynamic. Dealing with only "black and white" solutions and no self-reflection can strain the child unnecessarily.

A parent can make their child feel burdened with statements they view as loving, such as "I need you," "you give me a reason to live," or "you're my best friend." The blurred boundary can make it really hard for the role of parent and child to be clear.

There are even a lot of diversion tactics that emotionally immature people use to ensure they don't have to go deep or take responsibility for their actions. There are certain things to look out for, and here is a list to get you started:

- Laughing instead of talking or making a joke out of everything, especially when it feels very serious to you. A bit of humor is one thing, but constantly turning your issues and thoughts into a joke can feel very demeaning.

- Making an excuse not to talk *right now*—they're busy, stressed, or have a headache. They just don't seem to have the time for you, no matter when you go to them.

- They turn the conversation back to them and become overly defensive if you try to stop this. They are always the center of everything.

If you're still wondering if this applies to you, maybe you're still feeling a little confused about the upbringing you had. Flipping things over and looking at how emotionally *mature* parents work can help to clarify things:

- *Flexible Thinking:* Emotions are normal, everyone feels them, but emotionally mature parents can healthily handle problems when they come across them. They don't have rigid thinking controlling everything, which makes any slight change problematic. Rigid thinking can be seen when parents refuse to acknowledge that they might be wrong about something or that the schedule can change.

- *Experimental Behavior:* Emotionally mature adults can adapt their behavior to what's happening around them, swallowing pride and asking for help or adapting and changing behavior according to whatever they're faced with. Experimental parents understand that they don't know everything about parenting and are willing to try new rewards and punishments to see what suits their family best.

-

Understanding Context: We aren't always our best selves. Lack of sleep, a selection of issues all at once, or a new environment can affect our mood and how we are. Emotionally mature adults will understand that sometimes, your mood isn't about them. They won't jump to defensiveness and make your day worse. They will take a step back and first examine the whole situation.

Emotionally mature people are *willing* to take responsibility for their feelings, are *able* to hold empathy, and are *honest* about their thoughts and feelings.

These behaviors aren't always easy habits to break, but this isn't your job. You aren't here to break anyone else's cycles, just your own. You can't make someone else do the work. But recognizing these behaviors in your parents will give *you* the context to deal with situations that arise if you keep your parents in your life.

Remember, this book is all about *understanding* your parents but not trying to heal them. You must take this time to concentrate on yourself and grow internally. They are responsible for working on themselves, which they might not want to do. If so, you can only accept that and concentrate on you.

You can only control yourself, so why not hone that and work on it?

Not all emotionally immature parents are the same. If you want to learn more about the one you grew up with, let's go to the next chapter and do a much deeper dive. Knowing what sort of emotionally immature parents you have can assist you in understanding yourself and in moving forward.

Chapter 2: Types of Emotionally Immature Parents

Not all emotionally immature parents look the same, so people who study this behavior have created four categories. This might be a very oversimplified way to look at it, but it will also give you some clarity. Understanding your parents will allow you to understand yourself. So, please read on with an open mind and tailor this to what suits you and your situation.

Most studies done on emotional parents sort them into four main categories. You will likely recognize at least one of these categories in your own life and childhood.

Emotional Parents

Traits of emotional parents come from *feelings*. Small issues become massive upsets that impact everyone around them. These parents can swing from deep involvement in their child's life to sudden disinterest, which seems to come from nowhere. It's manipulation, as are many of their words: *"I must be the worst parent in the world then!"*

The instability and unpredictability can be *really* hard to deal with, especially if the emotional parent uses intoxicants to soothe them.

You can tell that your parent is emotionally immature if they display any of the following traits:

- They *always* come first. They are self-centered and expect everything to revolve around how they feel at that moment, no matter what anyone else is going through.

- Criticisms are *not* received well. These parents are rigid and convinced that they are always right.

- Defensiveness, sensitivity, and reactiveness are common in these parents, making it very difficult to approach them about anything.

- They expect others to cave to calm them down. They often get what they want because it's easier for everyone around them.

- They fear emotion and can't deal with their children's issues. They expect their children to just keep it to themselves.

- All of this can lead to mental struggles and substance abuse to control the endless rollercoaster of feelings.

Driven Parents

This parent might come across as the most "normal," showing a lot of investment in their child's life. But this investment isn't genuine interest; it's more control. This parent sees you as an extension of themselves and certainly doesn't look to fulfil your emotional needs.

If they see that their child does not value the same thing they do (i.e., academic success), it feels like a personal attack and can make them freak out.

You can tell your parent is driven to an unhealthy degree if they display any of the following traits:

- They demand obedience no matter what, and they will not be questioned about their commands.

- They never encourage choice and independence because the parent *always* wants to make the decisions. They think they know best and must dictate everything. They will even "help" without being asked.

- Manipulation happens through punishment, coercion, and negativity.

- Disappointment and shame are constant within the child because there is no empathy or concern for the child's emotional needs.

- There's no privacy and autonomy because the parent is always in control. The parents are *always right*, and their expectations *must* always be met.

Passive Parents

The passive parent avoids drama and conflict. To their children, they are often the favorite parent because they seem so much easier to get along with and don't limit much... but they also don't offer guidance when it comes to emotions. They don't stand up for their children if the other parent is doing something wrong, even if this is neglect or abuse.

"Children wisely know not to expect or ask for much help from these parents. While passive parents actually enjoy their children, have fun with them, and make them feel special, the children sense that their parents aren't really there for them in any essential way."

~ Lindsay Gibson, PsyD.

You can tell that your parent is passive if they display any of the following traits:

- There are no rules, or the rules are really flexible, which means they are often ignored or bypassed. This can lead to the sense of being nagged all the time.

- Your parents focus way too much on warmth and interaction but nothing deep. Any real emotions become overwhelming for them.

- Passive parents ask for their child's opinion all the time, almost as if they can't make a choice without their input. Some choices are good for children, but too much makes them feel too much like a burden.

- Avoidance behavior is often seen with these parents because they can't handle negative outcomes. Anything that might become problematic or cause confrontation is simply ignored. They can also try to be a buffer so their children never feel negative emotions, leaving them completely unable to cope with difficulties throughout their lives moving forward.

Rejecting Parents

This parent wants to be left alone, so they don't engage with their family very well at all. They rule over the house but will not make themselves uncomfortable for anyone else, even their children. They cope by minimizing problems and acquiescing, leaving their children feeling helpless and worthless.

You can tell that your parent is rejecting if they display any of the following traits:

- They make you feel like a burden; you never want to go to them with a problem because it feels like they have "enough on their plate" already. Children of rejecting parents learn to keep their emotions to themselves always.

- They break their child's trust over and over again until they become self-sufficient and command self-perfectionism.

- They demand too much, and nothing you ever do feels good enough for them. You can follow all their "rules," but it's never enough. There is a level of expectation that you will *never* be able to reach.

- They are judgmental and make their children feel unlovable. This can actually lead the child to seek out love and acceptance in unhealthy places.

- Rejecting parents are terrible at communication, and they are also not good at affection. But this isn't something that they will take criticism over. When confronted, the rejecting parent will shut down and refuse to acknowledge anything. They don't just ignore the needs of those around them; they often ignore their own healthier needs, as well.

As you can see from these categories, most of these parents operate from a place of ego. Their world centers around themselves, and everyone else is simply within their gravitational pull. The children these people raise can either follow in their footsteps and become very similar people and parents themselves, or they can become people pleasers to everyone they come across. The other option, of course, is to try to break the cycle: to become very different from everything you know and become a whole person.

This won't be an easy journey when you are battling an ego that has always been there and doesn't want to break, but that doesn't mean you can't do it. This is why it's time to focus on *you* for a change. You can attempt to open up communication with your parents about this, but until you've done all the healing yourself, chances are, it might get ugly. You need to rewrite the narrative for yourself and who you want to be.

When you do get to the point of open communication, here are some tips to make sure that you get the best out of the conversation:

- Study the way that others communicate to get some good tips. Look at their body language and the clear, concise language with which they speak. Use that for yourself so that when you talk, you emulate that. Clear questions and speaking should lead to much clearer answers.

- Speak calmly. Shouting never gets you anywhere and always causes communication to escalate to a place it doesn't need to go. Just because yelling has always been there doesn't mean it should be now. Speak softly, keep your tone considerate, and don't react to emotional prodding. If it gets to be too much, leave.

- Show that you are listening to them and doing so with empathy. It isn't always easy to understand the other person, but we speak more honestly when we feel heard.

- Make sure the time is right–don't try this on a stressful day or one that has already gone bad. Allow for silences, too, and give them time to process things.

- If it doesn't go well, try again another time. Don't push things too far, or you will only get disastrous results.

Just because a certain cycle has always been in your family–yes, you might find it didn't just start with your parent but has always been an issue–doesn't mean you can't break it. Many people these days are trying to break generational trauma to form better lives for themselves, and you can, too. The time is now!

No matter what type of parent you have, you can heal from them; you can move on and lead a better, healthier life, which is exactly what this book wants to help you with. In the next few chapters, we will look at the sources for this emotional immaturity and how you can use this knowledge to help yourself move on with your life.

The causes of this emotional immaturity can actually have a massive impact on what type of parent you have, and understanding this can be the first step to healing. So, in the next chapter, we can take a look into *why* your parent is the way they are. Understanding where their ego and trauma come from can create deeper empathy and understanding. Your parent isn't perfect either, but chances are, they have a story of their own to tell.

Chapter 3: What Causes Emotionally Immature Parents?

Maturity describes our final stage of growth, and immaturity means that hasn't quite happened yet; the growth is still in progress. This is easy to see and understand when it comes to physical growth, but spotting emotional maturity is much harder. That's probably why it's taken you a while to realize how unusual the situation was that you grew up in. We view our parents as older and wiser; we respect them and expect them to take care of us in the best way possible. But unfortunately, that isn't always what happens.

Sometimes, people aren't in the right headspace to become parents. They might not even realize it themselves until it's too late and the damage is already done. Now it's up to you to try to overcome it.

We have looked at how to spot these parents, but we haven't yet covered what causes parents to be this way. It isn't something that just *happens*, and discovering the root cause when it comes to your own parents can help you. It will highlight how this actually has nothing to do with you as a person.

It has much more to do with *them*.

Emotionally immature parents often don't have any coping techniques for regulating their nervous systems. They are so used to jumping from the ventral vagus nerve, surviving in "fight or flight" mode. Unfortunately, they have continued with the cycle and are having the same effect on their own children.

While it has not come from *you*, the children are the ones who suffer, which is why it's *really* important for you to be the one to break the cycle.

You aren't to blame for your parents, but you are the one who needs to change things. They started parenthood emotionally immature; *you* didn't do anything to deserve it. You also can't change it because, as previously stated, you can only focus on yourself.

This emotional immaturity can come from a number of different places. Understanding the source of the issues can be really useful when it comes to your own recovery because it can make you see why your childhood was the way it was.

Mental Health

This can be a huge factor in the way you were raised. Depression hasn't always been looked upon as something to take care of until recent years. For years, humans have treated it as self-inflicted and something to be ashamed of. That means our parents grew up in a world where they had to deal with their mental health issues alone, without therapy and medication.

That might not be their fault, but that doesn't diminish the effects it can have on a child. It provides an environmental risk in which a child has to survive. Depression can be a big part of the cycle and something that is passed down through generations, especially when there is no healing done along the way.

This is scary to think about. Some of the symptoms to look out for include:

- Tearfulness or excessive sadness.

- Irrational irritation toward the people around you.

- A sense that you can no longer be bothered to do the things that you used to love.

- No energy and constant tiredness; sleeping too much or not enough.

- A numbness–no feeling about anything.

- Trouble concentrating on anything.

- Decision-making suddenly becomes an almost impossible task.

- A change in eating habits–under or overeating, especially if this is linked to emotions.

- A vicious cycle of negative thoughts and feelings. Never feeling good enough, always stressed and worked up, unable to cope.

- Constant guilt and self-blame for anything happening around you.

- Anxiety spikes that seem to come from nowhere and last too long.

- Troubles bonding with other people.

There are many effects depression can have on the parents' children. Studies suggest that children who are raised by emotionally immature parents suffering from mental illness are at an increased risk of facing similar problems themselves: depression, anxiety disorders, OCD, eating issues, and many other issues.

Personality Disorders

Lack of emotional maturity can actually come from a more serious mental condition, such as borderline personality disorder. These parents fail to live up to society's expectations at a young age and in their parental role. They often struggle to find independence and self-reliance, so they can't find a sense of calm or peace.

Signs to look out for to spot this type of disorder include:

Paranoid personality disorder

- An intense distrust of those around them and a suspicion that everyone is against them.

- The belief that everyone is "out to get them" with absolutely no evidence of that and a refusal to acknowledge that there isn't any evidence.

- Always distrusting and not believing others, with no reason to do so.

- Secretive because of the fear that any information can be used against them.

-

Taking all remarks as personal attacks and finding meaning that just isn't there in words.

- An over-the-top, hostile reaction to anything they see as a threat or an attack.

- A grudge holder, especially if the other person doesn't even know that they have done something wrong.

- Constant suspicion that a romantic partner is cheating on them.

Schizoid personality disorder

- Loneliness and a refusal to actively engage with other people.

- Limited to no expression of emotions, even when extreme feelings are there.

- They take no pleasure in anything, especially things they used to enjoy.

- Social cues are always completely missed.

- People see this person as very cold and unfeeling.

- No interest in a romantic or sexual partner.

Schizotypal personality disorder

- Acts in a way that might be considered peculiar to others: the way they dress or act, the words they say, or the inflection in their voice.

- "Hearing" strange things, like whispers that aren't there.

- Little to no emotional response to things that should illicit feelings.

- Total discomfort with other people, bordering on social anxiety.

- Strange responses to others. Suspicious acting or behaving with ignorance.

- Odd thinking and beliefs–such as in their own magic.

- They find "hidden messages" that no one else will understand, something that is just for them.

Antisocial personality disorder

- Complete disregard for the feelings and needs of other people.

- A con man personality–lying to others and stealing from them.

- This may cause endless issues with the law.

- The boundaries of others are always violated and broken as if they are meaningless.

- Aggressive behavior can often border on or become violent.

- No regard for safety, whether it comes to themselves or other people.

- Odd and impulsive behavior, which can scare those around them.

- Often irresponsible without any concern for how this impacts others.

- No apologies or even remorse for their behavior.

Borderline personality disorder

- Risky behavior that can be seen as impulsive. This can be gambling, unsafe sex, drinking alcohol, or using substances, even putting themselves needlessly in danger.

- A terrible self-image, which can sometimes inflate to a very high degree.

- Their relationships, whether romantic or otherwise, are often far too intense and fleeting.

- A rollercoaster of emotions and an inability to regulate those feelings.

- Sadness bordering on self-harm and suicidal ideation.

- Attachment issues and a terrible fear of being left alone.

- A constant numbness or an emptiness inside that never really shifts.

- Explosive episodes of anger that often don't make much sense.

- Paranoia that comes and goes with stress.

Histrionic personality disorder

- They are constantly seeking attention and will do anything to get it. This includes provocative behavior, wild and irrational emotions, and constant "drama" in their lives.

- Will form strong opinions and stubbornly stick to them, ignoring any evidence that proves otherwise.

- Influenced by peer pressure and those in their lives. Often, their personality will match who they are with at that time.

- Emotions that fluctuate without any outward reason as to why.

- An intense concern with their self-image.

- Has a belief that relationships are intense and close but might actually be much more casual.

Narcissistic personality disorder

- A feeling of being special and better than other people—more knowledgeable and important.

- A deep desire for power, money, success, good looks... anything to add to their sense of self-importance.

- A complete failure to even acknowledge that others have feelings and needs because they simply aren't important.

- Exaggeration of who they are and what they have achieved, which is coupled with a constant need for praise.

- They are arrogant and expect everyone else to view them in the same way.

- Their expectations of other people are unrealistic and completely over the top, almost as if they deserve to have everything done for them.

Avoidant personality disorder

- Highly sensitive to anything perceived as rejection or even criticism.

- Troubles with socializing and being around other people, so they will avoid situations that require it, whether this be at work or in social situations.

- Dealing with other people comes with an intense shyness which borders on critical.

- A horrible fear of disapproval or being humiliated. They already feel "less than"–unattractive, etc.–so they don't want to draw attention to that.

Dependent personality disorder

- An irrational, unrealistic dependance on those around them, leading them to be clingy and submissive to those they think they need.

- A lack of self-confidence which leads to them fearing that they don't know how to be alone or look after themselves.

- They need constant reassurance.

- There's a real inability to make decisions or start projects without the input of others.

- They will often tolerate bad treatment because they are so scared of being left alone. They struggle with confrontation or even disagreement, so they simply avoid it as much as they can.

- They can't be without a romantic relationship.

Obsessive-compulsive personality disorder

- They have an irrational need to have everything organized and routine. This often means they can't enjoy things fully.

- They suffer from an extreme level of perfectionism that no one can achieve, which means they disappoint themselves often.

- They are controlling and can't delegate. They *need* to do everything themselves.

- They are rigid and stubborn in their beliefs. They will not hear anything different when it comes to their ideas and morals.

Having a parent with this sort of disorder can be particularly troubling and lead to some issues in the life of the child, who are likely to need to therapy to assist in resolving them. If you think this might be something you need to deal with, see if any of the following apply to you:

- Toxic Shame: parents with personality disorders pass the blame onto others, which leaves children feeling like they are always being blamed for things that are not their fault. Toxic shame comes from walking on eggshells and from having the blame and unhealthy emotions dumped on you.

- Codependency: individuality from a child is a threat to a parent with a personality disorder. Boundaries are blurred, and any threat to take you away from the parent can cause tantrums and endless issues.

- Identity Confusion: it can be really hard for a child who has a parent with personality disorder to develop their own personality and sense of self. Ideas and feelings are shut down, so it can be hard to express them moving forward.

- Stunted Emotional Development: living with a lot of conflict, or none at all, and passive aggressiveness instead stunts your development, especially if you have always been forced to push your own feelings to one side and present an image of "perfection" to the outside world.

Substance Abuse

A lot of unhealthy coping mechanisms come with emotional immaturity, and this can include substance abuse and alcoholism. This can be escapism and avoidant, especially when strong feelings are involved.

Concerted attempts have been made to relate personality factors to alcohol dependence, especially when you consider that people with addiction issues tend to need a lot of attention and expect a lot from the world; they react badly to failure, often wanting to block it out, and they also feel inadequate and take it out on other people.

It's likely you have realized by now if your parent has an addiction issue, but you may not have taken the time to reflect on how this affected you growing up. It might be a good idea to take the time to think about this and consider what you went through:

- The "all or nothing" idea that addicts often hold onto means they are unable to modulate emotional responses. This leaves the people around them walking on eggshells, not quite sure what's to come next.

- Addicts don't often have an accurate perspective on things, so frustration can quickly bubble over into something really intense and overwhelming.

- Delaying gratification and controlling impulses is something that addicts and emotionally immature people struggle with, which makes working towards goals very challenging. Anger comes from not being able to give up this instant gratification.

- This inability to control themselves often leads to harsh words being spoken or behaviors being carried out that normally wouldn't be, but an emotionally immature person struggles to hold themselves responsible for that.

There have been many studies on emotional immaturity and alcohol use, which is very insightful, especially if you're looking back at your childhood:

- Learned helplessness can be seen in emotionally immature parents, making the normal challenges of life feel impossible. Everyone else is left to pick up the pieces, and their self-esteem continues to sink.

- Pessimism follows this, and the person can only see the negative outlooks on everything. This affects their ability to form any kind of meaningful relationship.

- There is no time like the present... because they are

always reliving the past or panicking about what's to come. They are never active in the present moment or engaging with anyone properly–including their own children.

- The mood swings are severe and seemingly out of control. The high expectations emotionally immature people have don't help because tempers can flare easily when these expectations aren't met.

If you have grown up surrounded by addiction issues, you can feel very isolated, and it can actually lead you down the same path. As a cycle breaker, I'm sure that this is something you wish to avoid, but there may still be some effects that you need to examine:

- Lack of trust in yourself or those around you.

- Always very vigilant, to an excessive degree, in social situations.

- A terrible sensitivity to comments made by others, often reading into things that aren't there.

- Keeping to yourself and limiting what you share with others as a means of self-preservation.

- Self-perfectionism that often leads people to be miserable because these goals are unattainable.

- Putting the needs of others first, even to the detriment of yourself.

- Withdrawing to avoid conflict.

- Disconnecting from your feelings, especially the difficult ones like anger and sadness, and finding it hard to express these feelings appropriately. This also extends to struggling to cope with negative emotions in others.

- Seeking out escapist behaviors when times are tough.

- Black and white thinking; everything is either "all good" or "all bad."

- Finding crises and creating drama when there is nothing to worry about.

- A toleration for bad behavior in others because of a lack of self-esteem.

Studies have also shown that while each household suffering from addiction is different, there are often a set of unspoken rules that children learn to follow instinctively, including:

- *Rule One*: Keep all problems to yourself... what happens in the home, stays in the home. This secretiveness stops you from getting help and changing things.

- *Rule Two*: Keep your feelings inside; this will be something you learn when you are ignored and invalidated as you grow up.

- *Rule Three*: Don't bring others home to the unstable environment. Keep everyone at an arm's length.

- *Rule Four*: Seek perfection even though you will never be good enough. You will also never be validated.

- *Rule Five*: Don't be selfish; thinking of yourself will always be criticized and seen as selfish.

- *Rule Six*: Don't behave badly, even if the parent do. Your parents will often yell at you for doing the same things as them.

- *Rule Seven*: There is no play time. It's all about pleasing your parents.

- *Rule Eight*: Avoid conflict because that will lead your parents to drink more, and the vicious cycle will begin all over again.

Getting help to recover from this chaotic life is the first step towards becoming your own person. Therapy can assist with overcoming these ingrained habits, so you can start to live freely once more. If your parents are willing, family therapy can also be very beneficial.

Childhood Trauma

I have mentioned a few times in this book how this is a "cycle," and parents are often repeating the same patterns they learned when they were a child, which is why they can't always see that what they are doing is wrong.

Sometimes, because they aren't "as bad" as their own parents, they really can't see where you are coming from with your trauma. They believe that since they suffered more, you have nothing to complain about.

There are a lot of things that can be considered trauma, and there are also many signs to look out for. If you are unsure about your parents' backgrounds, and you do not feel okay asking them, then this list might be useful for you:

- Abuse: physical, emotional, mental, or even neglect. In childhood, this will impact everything going forward.

- Living in a home of domestic violence and constantly feeling unsafe.

- Bullying or being bullied. Both will cause trauma.

- Violence in their life: this can be personal or even in the community. There will still be an effect.

- Natural disasters impact those affected greatly. Often people will take years to recover.

- Grief: the loss of a loved one or even a serious incident. There will be lasting effects from this.

These incidents can have a negative impact on a person growing up, and sometimes, they might not even know it. But if this is something you're concerned about, some of the signs of PTSD include:

- Flashbacks during the day or even as nightmares.

- Avoidant behaviors that might not seem rational to other people.

- Mental health conditions, such as depression and anxiety disorders.

- Extreme emotions: anger, distrust, or withdrawal.

- Risky actions and self-destructive behaviors that scare people around them.

But the effect might be much smaller than that. They instead struggle with building emotional connections and relationships with other people, especially those closest to them. They also might not be able to control their emotions, which leads to intense anger, sadness, and dramatic mood swings all the time. There can even be physical health effects, such as heart problems or asthma.

If any of this trauma is left unresolved, there can be a ripple effect. It can impact everyone in the person's life. The past can resurface at any moment and show itself in many ways. Your emotionally immature parent has caused trauma for you, which means you also need to do some work... but reading this book is a great start in the right direction!

Unresolved Neurodiversity

Neurodiversity refers to how we interact with the world around us. There's no "right" or "wrong" way to do this, but Judy Singer, a sociologist who has autism, started talking about this more and used the associated terms in the late 1990s. Autism and ADHD are commonly known neurodivergent conditions which are much more commonly picked up on today than before.

Many adults are only just being diagnosed, which means that they have lived their whole lives without quite understanding how their brains connect with the world, especially when it comes to complex tasks, such as parenting.

We can also use the concepts of *rupture* and *repair* to better explain the effects of this.

Rupture and repair are psychological terms used when we talk about relationships in a family, especially our parents. It looks at the way trust is built through our attachment styles. There is a mutual trust that is built up over the years as you live and grow in a home together.

But this trust can be ruptured. Moments of disconnect will happen when trust is broken or when a parent prioritizes something else over their child. This happens with everyone. No parent is perfect, and no human can do everything right all the time...

So, this leaves room for the repair, and that is a time when a parent acknowledges they have done something wrong and apologize for it.

"Ruptures happen. Repairs also happen. This is a very positive thing, because children end up being more secure when they find that good things can follow bad things. We're not perfect, and if we were, we'd be setting our children up for severe disappointment in a world that is anything but perfect. Plus, we'd be preventing them from developing a resilient sense of self that trusts that mistakes are a normal – even healthy – part of genuine relationships."

– *Raising a Secure Child*, by Kent Hoffman, Bert Powell, & Glen Cooper

Since attunement is much harder with a neurodivergent parent, the rupture and repair cycle can be much more challenging. The communication and lifestyle are different, often leaving the child confused and frustrated. Routines can be complex, and they can be hard to understand. If you and your parents are both approaching the world differently, this means that everything is understood in a different way.

Without a diagnosis, it can be hard to confirm if neurodiversity is the issue, but if you suspect this might be the case and want to try communicating with your parent, here are some tips for you:

- Be very clear: don't use jokes or sarcasm because they won't be picked up.

- Use concise, short sentences, and never be too "wordy." The same applies to written communication.

- Be direct and try to use closed sentences. Avoid questions where you can.

We can also study this using the easily memorable acronym, APPLE:

- **A**sk to join: Use other cues and words, including body

language and facial expressions.

- **P**hysical proximity and volume: Put yourself in a place where you can hear and express yourself properly.

- **P**articipate: Ask questions and show interest in what's being talked about.

- **L**ay off self-criticism: Stay engaged in the present moment and tune out any negative thoughts.

- **E**njoy connecting with others: Appreciate the social connection and smile. Communication is a way to connect and build a bond with other people.

There are a lot of places where you can get help with this and for your parent, too, if they are willing and able. But if that isn't the case, please remember that it was never about you; it was all about their struggles with communication.

Lack of Self Awareness

Self-awareness is so important when it comes to regulating emotions. Without it, you don't stand a chance. If your parents have brought you up without it, then you might have noticed some of the signs:

- Emotionally out-of-touch: not recognizing their own emotions, or those of others, will make people speak or react inappropriately to things.

- Impulsive behavior: they don't think long about what they're about to do. This can lead to aggression, sexual promiscuity, drinking too much, driving recklessly, etc.

- Highly critical: they push their insecurities on other people to make themselves feel better. They also use positive reinforcement as a way to manipulate people rather than in a genuine way.

- Closed-off: they don't want feedback because they don't want to examine their behavior. Feedback is criticism, and while they can dish that out, they can't take it.

- Know-it-all: they often get stuck in vicious cycles because their arrogance makes them feel like they know more than everyone else.

- Drama seems to follow them: a lack of empathy and their constant defensiveness without looking inwards means they are always in a cloud of drama.

- Failing at coping: their mechanisms of coping are unhealthy and always backfire. For example, there is overspending, gambling, or drinking too much.

- Control is important: they believe they are the center of everything, so they must control how the world revolves around them.

- People pleasers: sometimes a lack of self-awareness can lead to a difficulty in saying "no" because validation makes them feel worthy.

- They can't let go of the past... but they also can't say sorry if they are the one in the wrong, ever.

If this is something you have developed due to your emotionally immature parents, then all hope is not lost. Here are some simple, great tips to get you started with your healing and self-awareness.

- Know what you're doing. Don't live life on autopilot any longer. Work on living mindfully so you are in the present moment, not stuck in the past or the future, missing the *right now.*

- Know what you're feeling. Stop suppressing your emotions in the hope that they will go away. Deal with your feelings, even the unpleasant ones.

- Know your own issues, dealing with your triggers and behaviors that might not be the best.

Self-awareness can force us to confront our emotional immaturity. It might not always be the most pleasant journey, but the end result will definitely be worth it. *Respond Rather than React.* Once you learn to do that, your life will be calmer and much more pleasant.

You will benefit most of all.

Now that we have a better understanding of why our parent became the way they are, we now need to examine the effect this has had on you. After all, as we've already established, you can't change *them*, but you can learn to react in a healthier way for yourself.

So, what effect did your childhood have on you? Read on for more. You didn't just survive your childhood; you came out affected from it in your childhood and your adulthood, as well. But don't worry; you *can* heal.

Part 2 - How Do Emotionally Immature Parents Affect Their Child?

Chapter 4: Effects in Childhood of Emotionally Immature Parents

So now that you know more about how your parents have been emotionally immature, it's time to look at how this might have affected you. I'm sure you will recognize yourself in some of these statements, so I hope this reassures you that you aren't alone. There are others out there who have suffered just as you have, but there are also many people who have gone on to heal, which is evidence that you can, as well.

There are smaller signs to look out for—things you might not have even noticed were strange growing up, but looking back, it's easy to see how and where your behavior came from and how:

- Loneliness: spending a lot of time alone or even feeling misunderstood. Growing up around others who haven't suffered like you can make that feeling of isolation fester. Alone time is easier because no one else understands.

- Dismissive: you have grown up dismissing your own feelings and emotions and maybe those of others, too. As long as basic physical needs are met, nothing else needs to be dealt with in quite the same way.

- Quiet and defensive: a need to self-protect is there all the time, so when someone has a different opinion, this can lead to children shutting down or getting angry.

But the effects can actually run much deeper than this, which is what we're going to look at in this chapter. A rollercoaster of emotions isn't a good environment for anyone to grow up in.

There is no denying that growing up with emotionally immature parents will have an effect on you. It can lead to emotional deregulation in children because they have never seen how to regulate their moods and deal with issues. They also had to put the moods of other people first all the time.

The signs of emotional dysregulation include:

- Deep depressive episodes and anxiety disorders that are life-altering.

- Excessive shame and anger that you cannot get rid of.

- All forms of self-harm–hurting yourself, using substances, risky behavior, sexual promiscuity, and eating disorders, to name just a few.

- Suicide thoughts.

- Issues with relationships and an inability to connect with others properly.

- A low self-worth because your feelings have never been considered important.

- Lack of trust in yourself and other people.

- An inability to live up to your potential because you are too focused on other people.

The causes of this emotional deregulation come from the trauma experienced in early childhood. The early years of our lives are the most critical period in our development, so if our needs aren't met during that time, it can have a long-term effect. This doesn't just refer to our physical needs, although we do need those met, as well. It's our emotions, too.

If our feelings are constantly rejected, judged, or invalidated, then our neurotransmitters are affected. They can no longer put the brakes on our emotions, so this function effectively switches off. We end up existing in survival mode and constantly struggle.

This can lead to all kinds of disorders, including:

- Post-traumatic stress disorder: can show itself with flashbacks, anxious disorders, uncontrollable negativity and self-doubt, dissociation, and emotional numbing.

- Borderline personality disorder: causes problems with normal, everyday tasks. This affects our self-esteem, emotional and behavioral management, and leads to unstable relationships.

- Frontal lobe disorders: these can lead to impulsive decision-making, challenges with motivation, and an inability to connect properly.

- Obsessive-compulsive disorder: this shows itself in streams of intrusive, life-changing thoughts.

It might feel a little bit overwhelming to read this and to think it might apply to you, but it doesn't have to be. There *are* plenty of ways in which you can heal; you just need to work out what is right for you:

- Therapy: cognitive-behavioral therapy uses mindfulness and behavior change to successfully help with emotional dysregulation.

- Medication: antidepressants and other medication can

help stabilize you, so if this is the route you take, make sure you find the tablet that's right for you.

- DBT: dialectical behavioral therapy teaches you how to manage yourself and navigate the world properly.

- Diet and exercise: self-care is great for everyone at all times, so making sure that you are moving well and getting the right nutrients and vitamins will assist you in lifting up your mood.

- Doctors can also help with emotional regulation training and check to see if you have any underlying conditions.

Getting help is nothing to be ashamed of, especially when you have grown up in a difficult environment. Reaching out is actually the most difficult step. Everything doesn't need to work out just as you think it's going to, either; it's often by trial that you will find the solution that suits *you*. Here are some signs to look for.:

- Excessive crying: emotions that don't seem to have a justified reason behind it or crying that lasts longer or is more intense than what is situationally appropriate can be something to look further into, especially if there's irrational fear involved or suicide ideation.

- Social issues: problems with interacting with others because of their extreme emotions need to be looked at. Puberty may exacerbate this, but it'll definitely be noticed beforehand.

- Mood swings: it isn't just the negative emotions that are extreme but the positive ones, too. Impulsivity and reckless behavior are common.

If you're worried about someone in your life, there might be many reasons why emotional deregulation has occurred. You don't necessarily have to jump to the conclusion that you have done something wrong. It isn't always emotional immaturity. The way that life is today can have an impact:

- Too much waiting: children these days spend a lot of time sitting in the car or waiting at restaurants for food, which makes them impatient and easily irritable.

- Their time is organized: children don't have enough time to be bored and amuse themselves. They have organized clubs, a lot of homework, helicopter parents watching their every move, and schedules to fit in. This leaves very little time for independent thinking.

- Technology: the main way to pass the time these days isn't playing outside and getting rid of excess energy; it's zoning out in front of the television or playing on screens instead.

- Rushing: life is busy, and we're always rushing from one place to the next to fit everything in. There's no time to do the simple things like watching the clouds go by.

While there is no way to change the naturally fast-paced nature of life, you can do some things to help your children. You can take fewer car rides and sign up for fewer activities. Slow down and unplug when possible. Head outdoors if you can.

If you're reading this book because you are worried about someone else—a child, in particular —and this chapter has you more convinced, then please reach out for help, especially if you notice any of these symptoms:

- Extreme moodiness and mood swings.

- Don't know how to take the blame or take the blame for everything.

- They treat necessities as privileges because that's how their parents treat them.

- They have no self-worth because of the criticism they always suffer.

- They show no emotions or extreme emotions.

- There is extreme sibling rivalry.

- Bullying and lashing out at others.

- They look and seem neglected and are struggling to get along with kids their own age.

Look for local charities or members of authority to speak to about this and get the child help, especially if this is extreme. The sooner it's dealt with, the easier healing will be.

But it wasn't just your childhood affected. Your adulthood has been impacted. as well, which is why you are where you are, reading this book for advice. That's what you need to change, which is why you bought this book in the first place. So, keep reading to discover how you got to where you are now.

Chapter 5: Effects in Adulthood of Emotionally Immature Parents

Your adult years are more dominated by your childhood than you realize. It's only when you start to unpack everything that's happened to you and realize how it's still festering that you can move on from it and become a much more well-rounded person.

Your adulthood will also likely be affected by the parents you grew up with, especially if they were emotionally immature. Some of the most common lingering issues have been noted as:

- Remaining excessive feelings, including anger and sadness, or attachment issues and a fear of moving on with your life.

- Experiencing shame or guilt for being unhappy or

happy.

- Being over-sensitive to how those around you are feeling.

- An inability to trust yourself and believe in your own instincts.

- No self-esteem and a sense of being locked in by your parents because of how you were forced to live with them growing up.

Here are four ways your emotionally immature parents may have impacted you and how they have made you feel—not just at the time you were living under their roof but now, as well. Don't just dismiss these ideas before you have really read through them to see if they apply to you:

Unimportant

If you have always been forced to put the feelings of others first, pushing your own to the side, then that's something that will have likely followed you into adulthood. If you still have contact with your parents, you likely still treat them like they are a priority.

This will have also affected your other relationships because you feel responsible for the way others are feeling. Because you can't change the way others are feeling, this will likely leave you with a sense of helplessness, as well.

It's a vicious cycle that you need to escape from, but you *can* escape from it. Later in this book, we will discuss techniques that can assist you with putting your own feelings first for a change and working out exactly how you feel.

Unsafe

If your needs are never met, you grow up feeling safe expressing them. If you're dismissed or met with negativity, chances are, you learned to bottle everything up instead. You might still find it really hard to express yourself.

Learning how to communicate effectively and express yourself also means getting rid of the guilt and shame attached to sharing how you feel. It will be a process that allows people to get closer to you by the end.

Imagine it. Think about the simple act of telling someone how you feel honestly and being listened to without judgment. I promise you that there are people like that in your life; you just need to find ways to open up to them. Being vulnerable is scary, but it's so rewarding when you build those deeper and more fulfilling bonds with the people in your life.

Unresolved

When someone refuses to acknowledge that they have done something wrong, it can leave people with unresolved feelings. Not having the chance to express your own feelings and have any kind of closure can be really frustrating. It can leave a deep anger within you that's hard to shake off. But taking a step back from that anger is also freeing.

In life, not everything will be resolved. It's one of those unfortunate things that we simply cannot control. Accepting that will allow you to accept a part of yourself.

If you've learned that saying sorry is a weakness or that *you* must be the one to take the blame for everything, it's likely something you've carried into adulthood with you.

You need to untangle this line of thinking to let go of the lingering unhappiness that has stuck with you. I bet once you start untangling these feelings, you will start to let go of the past in ways you couldn't imagine.

Unaware

Parents walk around, always triggered, because they don't take the time to look inwards and see what might be making them feel a certain way. Even offering them a solution doesn't help things. This lack of self-awareness is terrible for the people around them because they have to be on extra high alert to overcompensate for that.

This has obviously left you walking on eggshells around them and likely unable to form proper bonds with others. Because of their lack of self-awareness, chances are, you have acute self-awareness to make up for it.

This will have also made you grow up before your time, leaving you in the adult role when you should have been allowed to be a child. Missing out on childhood is sad, and it's a time in life that you may need to grieve about. If that's the case, take a step back and do that. Maybe even speak to a therapist about it because the past doesn't need to hold you back forever.

It's not nice to confront our faults head-on, but accepting whom we have become is the first step to moving away from them. Plus, I hope this book has helped you to see that none of these things are your fault. You aren't to blame for where your life has gone because your childhood left you without basic coping skills.

Now that isn't to say you can step away from self-blame completely. We all have to take accountability for our mistakes, so we can heal. We all know that we need to do the work on ourselves because no one is perfect. There are always changes that can be made, but ridding yourself of at least some guilt can lift a weight off your shoulders and help you to keep going.

Here are some other things to look out for in your adult life to see how you have been impacted by your childhood. You are likely to recognize some of areas that you will definitely need to work on during your healing journey.

- Dysfunctional relationships: never seeing a healthy relationship often leaves us not sure of what the red flags are that we should be looking out for. We might even find ourselves attracted to similar toxic behaviors in partners and friends.

- Fear of abandonment: without a strong base of parental love, we grow attachment issues which can either make us clingy or withdrawn, pushing people away.

- Arrogant traits: surviving with emotionally immature parents can even lead us to grow up to be self-centered and a little narcissistic, just like them.

- Lack of identity: there is no time to grow and discover who we are and what our moral anchor is. This takes time to develop, and it's something you have to do actively once you're an adult.

- Hopelessness: with no support, joy and hope gets lost along the way.

But don't worry; there are a lot of ways to help you recover from, so it isn't hopeless. Here are some tips to get you started:

- Set healthy boundaries with your parents: not every-thing has to result in an emotional blow up, especially if you learn to love and accept your parents for who they are without trying to change them. You need to express these boundaries clearly, and make sure there are consequences if and when they are broken. It might not be easy for your parents to accept these boundaries at first, but if they want to keep a relationship with you, they will eventually learn to respect it. You must communicate well and always remind people of those boundaries. You must also not be afraid to say no.

- Treat your parents like adults: keeping the peace is fine... to an extent, but your parents won't ever really get to know you if you don't give them the fullness of who you are. Don't let them shame you into thinking that *you* aren't good enough.

- Use empathy: when trying to establish these bound-aries and revealing your true self, you may disappoint and upset your parents. While you might not agree with those feelings, acknowledging them aloud will lead to a better conversation about this. You might even find a way to have a healthy back-and-forth where you both feel understood.

Research has actually developed what they refer to as the Maturity Awareness Approach when it comes to dealing with your emotionally immature parents as an adult yourself, especially if you are struggling to be heard or set boundaries:

1. Use Your Observer Mind

Detach yourself emotionally from your parents, and simply observe them. Use your thinking and switch off your emotional reactions. This makes you a survivor rather than a victim; you can watch their selfishness from afar rather than getting caught up in it.

No longer needing their approval will be incredibly freeing for you. It will be a way of cutting those apron strings and finally becoming a full person all on your own.

2. Express and Then Let Go

When you get to the stage where you realize that you aren't really being listened to, the only thing you can do is clearly state what you need to say calmly and then let it go, no matter what they say back. It's not the easiest thing to do, especially when we are used to getting all tangled up in our feelings and emotions, but it's a skill we need to hone to move forward.

Once they learn that they can no longer get the desired reaction out of you, they will be forced to change to meet your strength. However, this change might not always be positive.

3. Focus on the Outcome, Not the Relationship

There isn't any way that a relationship with an emotionally immature parent will ever be fair, so instead of worrying about ways to make things better, focus on the bigger picture. You might not get that apology even if you were hurt, but if you want to keep a surface level relationship going, then concentrate on that. No one is forcing you to be completely open about yourself with your parents just because they are family. Let them talk about whatever they want and keep what you want to for the healthier people in your life.

4. Manage, Don't Engage

While focusing on the outcome, keep that end goal in mind no matter what. Use that to manage conversations rather than getting sidetracked by petty arguments and silly distractions, especially when you are talking about something serious and meaningful to you.

Sometimes, things become a little more serious, and you might need to really consider the contact that you have with your parents. Cutting them off completely *is* an option, but since it's

one that comes with a heavy burden of sorrow and loss, here are
some other suggestions that you might wish to consider first:

- Cordial contact: keeping a superficial relationship
  with your family requires strength, but you will soon
  see the benefits of keeping your emotions out of it.

- Low contact: this means you only see your parents at
  specific occasions, such as holidays, set by you. This
  time might be anxiety inducing, but if it works for you,
  always keep the control.

- Measured contact: firmly set your boundaries and
  refuse to have them broken despite any push back you
  might suffer.

- No contact: this means cutting your family out completely. It's the hard choice to make, but for some people, it's the only healthy way for them to move forward.
  After years of not putting yourself first, it might finally
  be time to.

- Reconciliation after estrangement: sometimes, you
  might come back to one another, but make sure your
  boundaries are always clear.

If all of these options feel a little heavy to begin with, then consider some small steps in the right direction. These might be simpler ways to start you off:

- Stop pleasing them: you can't please emotionally immature parents while also focusing on yourself. So, focus on *you* for a change. Don't always be at their beck and call, don't always work around *them*, and make sure your boundaries are clear.

- Stop changing them: You can't change emotionally immature people; they have to focus on changing themselves. The only person under your control is you.

- Stop sharing with them: start keeping things to yourself if you don't feel safe sharing with your parents. You don't have to give all of yourself over to them. Keep some of yourself for you.

- Always have an exit strategy: make sure you always have an excuse to leave when you're with your parents, so when communication breaks down or things begin to sour, you can protect yourself.

As long as you keep looking after yourself and prioritizing what you need for a change, you will be working toward a brighter and happier future. If you're looking for some ideas of what to do for your mental health and self-care, here are some good ones. Some of them are big, and some are much smaller, but they will all give you a good boost:

- Put sleep first: Your immune system will thank you for it, as will your mood. You can't be emotionally and physically at your best without proper sleep.

- Know Your Stress: Start to pay attention to yourself and what you look like when you're stressed and overwhelmed. When you start to act this way, it's time for self-care.

- Exercise: Working out really does help because it boosts endorphins, your happy chemicals, and helps with your focus and sleep. This doesn't have to be a hardcore gym work out; it can be a bit of yoga or even silly dancing to your favorite music. Just get your body moving.

- Utilize nature: There is Japanese practice called "shin-rin-yoku," which is sometimes referred to as "forest bathing." This is taking a walk with nature and breathing in the fresh, sweet air, which helps you calm your nervous system and rest.

- Play games: Play something that makes you smile, because a relaxing activity like a game can do wonders for your mindset. The same can be said for baking, running, or drawing... anything you enjoy doing.

- Stop snacking: Not fully. Don't put limits on yourself; instead focus on mindfully eating so you're getting the best out of your snacking experience. Pick high protein snacks or fruit and veggies for energy, as well.

- Try decaf: Caffeine is known for affecting your nervous system and sleep patterns. Late at night, trying a decaf might change more than you notice.

- Remember Gratitude: When times are tough, remember what you have in your life to be happy about. Journal these things, so you always have something to look back on. It can also be helpful to make note of things that don't make you feel so good, so you can work out if it's worth investing your energy in.

- Practice Positivity: Try talking to yourself kindlier, and pick up on the things that you do well. The kinder you are to yourself, the less of a weight you will have on you. Repetition is important, as well.

- Breathe Better: Breathing in a more mindful way with diaphragm breathing or alternate nostril breathing can help you center yourself. If this works well for you, practice other mindfulness exercises.

- Use the Arts: Music, books, TV... take some time to do something that you love. You can even take a whole vacation day to sit back and just enjoy being you—in a bubble bath with an audiobook, or with whatever you love.

- Social connection Reaching out to a healthy person in your life, such as a good friend or another family member, can lift your mood tenfold. Maybe even meet that friend because talking in person and having the chance to hug them can always make you smile.

- Massage: Having a massage has proven benefits when it comes to calming down and making you feel better. It gets you out of "fight or flight" mode.

- Get offline: Social media and the news don't always make us feel better, so sometimes it's better to disconnect from the online world. The offline world has a lot to offer, as well.

- Treat yourself: You can purchase something new, like a new dress or even a chocolate bar. Maybe take a hot bath or do some at-home spa treatments, just something to make you feel better.

- Get organized: A cluttered house or messy finances mess with your mind. If you have the time, get things cleared out and see how much better you feel afterward.

- Try something new: Learn a language or cultivate a home garden, something to keep your mind focused and make you smile.

Trying different things can help you find out what works best for you. Remember what makes you feel better, so the next time you're struggling, you know what to go back to. We are all unique, and there is no "one size fits all" approach to healing, so you have to focus on what works for you.

So, now you're much more knowledgeable about how your childhood has impacted you and why you are the way you are. Great, but what now? How does this help you? What do you do to move on with your life? The next section of the book will help you heal and move on. Why wait any longer? The focus on *you* has only just begun. Now you need to take that further and work with what you have.

Part 3 - Healing From Emotionally Immature Parents

Chapter 6: Improving Emotion Regulation Skills

N ow it's time to look at how you can recover from everything you have been through in your life and see all you can do to move on with your life. Because emotionally immature parents don't have to affect your whole life, they don't have to impact you forever. You *can* move on and have a healthy existence from here on out, which this chapter will help you with.

We can't avoid emotions; they are a massive part of everyday life. That's the first thing we need to accept. It's tempting to try to shut down our emotions because of how they affected us, but shoving everything down isn't the answer either. More than that, we shouldn't avoid our emotions because avoidance isn't healthy—even negative emotions. Allowing yourself to feel them without letting them consume you is the best way to live your life. It's the most freeing way to exist.

But if you have been surrounded by emotionally immature people for large periods of your life, it might not be the easiest thing to do. Regulating and experiencing your emotions in a positive way is something you need to work on. It's challenging but rewarding work that will allow you to finally move on from your past.

So, where do you even begin? If it's not something you have ever done before, identifying and seeking out your emotions can be challenging. It can feel like our brains are a silly mess with emotions running wild. It can seem like everything is intertwined, so there is no way to untangle that mess.

But that isn't the case—not at all. It just takes a little bit of focus and work. Once you start taking note of what's going on in your brain and start labeling these emotions, you'll find that you don't get caught up in it after all.

If this is something you're brand new to, start off simple—really simple. As in, just concentrate. Take time every day to notice what's going on in your body.

- Try it right now. How are you feeling? Give that emotion a name. Are you worried? Scared? Happy? Proud of yourself for taking these big steps in life? Once you name it, you'll almost feel a separation from it.

- To get started, you can even try tracking just one emotion. Pick anger or happiness, something that's strong, and you notice every time you feel it.

- Once you start noticing how often you feel a particular emotion, you can start paying attention to the triggers. What happens just before you feel it? Did someone annoy you? Or did someone else do something nice, making you smile? You might start to see patterns in your day and your emotions.

- Keep a journal. It can also be useful to write everything down, to keep track of all of your emotions, or at least one of them. Just really take control of everything.

- Once you know what leads to your emotions and how certain events make you feel, you can also take a moment to digest the emotions and learn how to process them better.

It's also important to start to see how your emotions don't just affect what's going on in your mind because it isn't just your mind that's affected. There is actually a cycle. The *Thoughts – Feelings – Behavior* cycle. If you have done any therapy, this might be a diagram you have already seen, but if not, take a moment to look at this and consider how it might relate to you and your situation:

Now, just looking at this out of context might not make a lot of sense, but if we put it into a situation that could be found in your everyday life, it might start to be easier for you to understand.

Say you find yourself in a situation at work where you're finding a particular task challenging for whatever reason. The cycle can start to look a little like this:

This is a very simplistic way of looking at it, but there are other things that you might notice, as well:

- Negative, self-hating thoughts make *everything* feel much harder, not just the particular task at hand. This can also pile on other life problems. You might start thinking about how empty your bank account is or how you left the house a mess, giving you "evidence" that you're a failure.

- Feelings inside the body, including heat, heart racing, shortness of breath, and dizziness.

- Behavior that involves alienating other people and isolating yourself.

You can see how the cycle feeds on itself, making everything feel so much worse. This is why it can feel messy, like you will never climb out of it because everything is spiraling and piling on top of one another. It's good to take note of all of this, *but* it's important to know that this isn't *all* negative. A more positive cycle can look like this:

This is where a feelings journal can help. You can even take to drawing the cycle in your journal to see how things are affecting you in more depth. It's especially important to take note of the physical effects these feelings and thoughts are having on your body. The anxiety of a racing heart and shortness of breath can make everything feel so much worse, but actually, that's your body's fight-or-flight response to negative thoughts and feelings.

You may have heard of *fight or flight* before, but if not, learning about it will also be useful, especially for someone who has grown up with emotionally immature parents. That leaves a person basically living in survival mode. Your body is so used to perceived threats because life has never felt calm or in control. It's an automatic physiological reaction to an event that is perceived as stressful or frightening, which means your body is preparing for danger as serious as a bear attack to help you *survive.*

Signs of *fight or flight* include fast, shallow breathing, sweatiness, dizziness, negativity, tunnel vision, muscle tension, body weakness, trembling, butterflies, fear, a need to urinate, pounding heart, and dry mouth, to name just a few.

This diagram shows some of what you might feel in *fight or flight* verses *rest and digest,* which is the state the body is supposed to be in:

Rest and Digest

- Easy breathing

- Light movements

- Clear sensory awareness

- Good weight distribution

- Steady heart rate

- Endorphins (happy chemicals) released

Fight or Flight

- Fast shallow breaths

- Quick and nervous movements

- Limited vision

- Awkward painful muscles through the feet

- Pounding heart and high blood pressure

- Cortisol (stress chemicals) released

If this is something you think you have suffered throughout your life, don't panic. This isn't a permanent state of being. You can change things for yourself. You *can* make things better. People have done it; there are many success stories about this, and you yourself can become one of these success stories.

Moving out of this "survival mode" is possible and starts with a little bit of self-reflection. In fact, many sources tell you that the first step is actually acknowledging that you're in survival mode. Taking note of where you are in life and your current head space allows you the freedom to move on from that. You can then move toward the next steps, which includes learning how to take care of yourself and asking for help if you need it.

If "taking care of yourself" is a little too vague of a statement, and you have absolutely no idea where to begin, here are some tips to get you started. Because once you care for *you*, everything else feels just a little bit easier:

- Exercise: just thirty minutes of movement a day can have a massive impact on you. It doesn't have to be anything strenuous if you aren't up for that; even walking counts, and it also doesn't have to be thirty minutes all at once. Even five-minute increments throughout your normal schedule will do you wonders.

- Healthy eating: this aids your digestive system, which impacts your nervous system more than you think. Plus, your focus and energy levels will rise significantly.

- Sleep well: without a proper sleep schedule, none of us can function properly. You need a schedule and regular hours for your body to calm down, rest, and digest.

- Relax: try something calming, meditate or listen to music, or sit with nature and just *be*—anything to stop your racing mind for a moment and just live in the present moment.

- Try having goals: give yourself something positive to aim for, something that will make you feel good about yourself, allowing your body to stop fighting invisible threats for just a little while.

- Connect well: keep in touch with the people who bring joy to your life, and spend happy moments with them. Always practice gratitude when you're with these people to remind yourself that it isn't all bad.

Now, these tips might seem very basic and not enough to help you. I'm not saying these will cure everything; they are just some tips to get you started. Picking up ways that you can help yourself will make it easier for you to do the work, even if you end up in therapy. But you may wish to dig deeper into understanding your emotions and how to deal with them, which is what we will look into next.

As this chapter has shown you so far, the way we normally recognize our emotions is through the effect it has on us and how this impacts our behavior. But doing some work to identify those feelings, write them down, and label them will give you some distance from them. But what do you do with that information?

The answer is learning how to regulate them, which is something you won't have seen in your childhood because it isn't something your emotionally immature parents ever did. It's a skill you need to learn on your own. This won't be easy, of course, because you're battling with your natural, in-built *fight or flight* system, which you have relied on for years, and you are also dealing with your prefrontal cortex, which is the part of your brain that makes rational decisions.

By not having your emotions responded to when you were a child, this part of the brain did not develop as it should have. If this is something you're worried about, some signs of this include:

- abrupt mood swings with little triggers

- binge eating or eating disorders

- crying spells and emotional outbursts

- persistent interpersonal conflict in the workplace or at home

- aggressive or violent outbursts

- self-harm or other self-sabotaging behavior

- substance use disorder, drugs, or alcohol.

- little tolerance for frustration

This part at the front of the brain is responsible for keeping you rational and aiding your decision-making. But if you're having issues with that, there are some exercises that can help you. According to research, it can even help to simply embrace and accept the following statements:

- Life isn't supposed to be fair.

- Goalposts move in life, and not always for a rational reason.

- Nothing is guaranteed.

- You *can* find ways to cope with what life throws at you.

- Nothing lasts forever.

- Disappointments are lessons and need perspective.

- Happiness can be found anywhere.

- You can't control what happens to you, but you can control how you react to it.

- Every day is a gift.

Now you might not be *there* yet, but it's definitely something to start telling yourself, perhaps in the morning to get you through each day. Learning how to soothe your nervous system can also be incredibly beneficial.

Calming your body down will help to calm your brain and allow you to start detangling yourself from that vicious cycle before it takes control of you. You can:

- Take a cold shower or hold an ice cube in your hand to

cool the burning heat in your body.

- Move gently to music or simply sway side-to-side for a couple of moments. Concentrate on those movements for a moment.

- Put your hand on your heart or the heart of someone else, maybe even a pet, and focus on the heartbeats.

As you can see, this all involves putting some distance between yourself and the emotion, giving yourself a bit of space to prevent thoughts and behaviors from embracing the cycle. This space will allow you to finally start seeing everything a little clearer, so you can make more rational decisions.

Healing the prefrontal cortex part of your brain will take some work, but it's also extremely beneficial to you moving forward in your life. Emotionally mature people all know how to control their emotions so they can process them properly and act in a way that doesn't have lasting damage on their life and relationships. After living a life where this has been a constant issue for you, isn't this something you want to try? For yourself?

Because remember, in this book, we're focusing on *you,* which is something that you haven't done for a very long time. Maybe not ever. Taking a look at some of the benefits of self-regulation might give you the boost you need:

- Your behavior will be more in line with your core values.

- You'll be able to calm yourself down before reaction and even cheer yourself up if you're feeling down.

- Open and honest communication will be much easier for you, improving all the relationships in your life.

- You will be more capable, using effort much more effectively. Your best intentions will remain at the forefront of your mind always.

- You'll be more flexible and able to handle change when it comes your way. Challenges will become opportunities instead of obstacles.

- You will find it much easier to see the good in others.

- You will feel more in control of your life and what happens around you.

In that last section, I talked about "core values." These are something we all hold dear, even if we haven't actively identified them. They are our beliefs that drive us forward through life, even if we sometimes push them to the back of our mind. These values are always there and are influenced by our life's experiences.

Identifying and labeling these core values is essential in any healing journey because it gives us aim; we can target our goals toward them and make sure we're living the life we want to be living. Here is a list of typical core values people pick out, so take a look through and highlight any that relate to you:

- Achievement

- Ambition

- Care

- Charity

- Collaboration

- Creativity

- Curiosity

- Dependability

- Empathy

- Encouragement

- Enthusiasm

- Ethics

- Excellence

- Fairness

- Family

- Friendships

- Flexibility

- Freedom

- Fun

- Generosity

- Growth

- Happiness

- Health

- Honesty

- Humor

- Individuality

- Innovation

- Intelligence

- Intuition

- Joy

- Kindness

- Knowledge

- Leadership

- Learning

- Love

- Loyalty

- Making a difference

- Motivation

- Optimism

- Open-mindedness

- Passion

- Perfection

- Performance

- Personal development

- Popularity

- Power

- Professionalism

- Punctuality

- Quality

- Recognition

- Relationships

- Reliability

- Resilience

- Risk-taking

- Safety

- Security

- Self-control

- Service

- Spirituality

- Stability

- Success

- Thankfulness

- Traditionalism

- Understanding

- Wealth

- Well-being

- Wisdom

Which from that list apply to your life and what you want from your existence? While you do this, consider people you admire and the experiences that you've had in life which have caused these to be the values you highlighted. Your parents may be considered in this, but don't put their core values ahead of your own. This is all about *you*.

Also consider the emotions, thoughts, and behaviors surrounding these values. How do they impact you in a positive way? If they don't, perhaps they aren't what you need in your life after all. Working toward positivity and happiness is extremely important here.

Once you have done this, try grouping the values into similar groups to try to identify a theme. This can help you narrow these values down to a few core ones that you always want to work toward. Knowing your core values can give you something to strive toward and can assist you with your behaviors moving on. It can even help to control your thoughts and emotions, leading to you regulating them much better.

However, if regulating emotions is something you're struggling with, and nothing so far has worked, it might be time to try something a little deeper. Here are tips for you to help improve your emotion regulation skills:

- Create Space: when the emotions rush over us, it can be hard not to get swallowed up by those feelings. Give yourself a moment to breathe before you react to something. The space doesn't have to be physical; it can simply be a place in your brain.

- Pay Attention: notice how you're feeling. Notice how your emotions affect you physically. Anxiety might give you a stomachache or anger a tight chest. Picking up on this will help to separate yourself from your feelings. To create even more distance, name the feeling and the sensations. This will help you to accept them.

- See Triggers: once you spot what triggers you and how you feel before you explode, this self-awareness can assist you with all aspects of life.

- Identify Thoughts: just because your brain tells you something, it doesn't mean it's true. Thinking everyone hates you because no one has reached out for a while is just a story your brain has concocted. They might just be busy in their own lives.

- Self-Compassion: practice this positivity in your life, treating yourself with the sort of kindness that you would the people you love.

- Have a Routine: this can always help you because focusing on where you need to be and when will prevent you from getting caught up in the thoughts, feelings, and behaviors cycle.

You can even think about this in relation to your parents and apply this by:

- Step out of your rescuer role: you are not in charge of someone else's life and the way that they feel. You have become more consumed with their lives than your own, which is very unhealthy for you.

- Sidestep the pressure: when things get too much, there's nothing wrong with slipping out and escaping to protect yourself.

- Limit yourself: don't spend too much time with your parents and set your own boundaries for how long you will be with them. This is like creating a space for yourself, but one away from the toxic people in your life.

There are also a number of suggestions which can help you parent your own children when you're recovering from your own emotional immaturity. These are practical skills that can assist you on a day-to-day basis to make better choices for you and your own family.

- Situation selection: this is picking and choosing to make sure you aren't trigged by people or places. Build your day around invoking positive emotions. For example, if you're planning a day out with your children but know a long drive causes fights and stresses you out, choose an activity that doesn't involve much of a drive.

- Situation modification: sometimes you can't pick where you are and what you're doing, but you do have the control over how you handle the moment. So, if you're stuck at home and can't go anywhere, think of activities you can all do that won't lead to stress and anger.

- Attention deployment: there are times when you can't even modify your situation, for example, if you're in a work meeting and get irritated because of the time it's taking. Instead of getting caught up in your emotions, focus your attention on something else. Think about something that makes you happy for a moment.

- Cognitive change: instead of refocusing your attention, try to see the situation that's stressing you out from another angle. If your child is whining and won't stop, take a moment and wonder why they are feeling so disconnected from you.

- Response modulation: breathe to cool down the heat in your body the moment it hits.

Mindfulness will often be recommended by health specialists to help you get a better grip on your emotions. Now, this is something which can be a book on its own, but to get you started with this practice, just to see if it's something that will work for you, try these simple exercises:

- Pay attention. Take time to notice what's around you. Note what affects all your senses. What can you see? Smell? Taste? Hear? Feel? Invoke everything within you.

- Live in the moment. Don't worry about the past or the future. Think about this moment *right now* and focus on everything happening within in.

- Accept yourself. Be kinder to yourself. Speak to yourself the way you would your best friend.

- Focus on your breathing. Feel your breath enter through your nose and exit through your mouth. This is more important than any thoughts plaguing your brain right now.

- Body scan meditation. Focus on each part of your body and note what sensations are there. See how these sensations make you feel and what they might be related to.

- Sitting meditation. Find somewhere peaceful to sit while you focus on your breathing and the present moment.

- Walking meditation. Feel your feet touch the ground, the air rushing over you, and the birds tweeting. Focus on the moment; there's nothing else to worry about right now.

These will help you get out of your emotions for a moment and focus on what else is happening around you. Mindfulness can even assist you in regaining control of your life because it allows you to think of everything in a new manner.

If this is something that you find works well for you, dig deeper into mindfulness. Many scientific studies have looked into this and proven how effective it can be, which is why it's now often offered by medical professionals.

These studies show that mindfulness can actually change your brain, healing the parts of yourself that have been damaged throughout life. Even people who start off the most skeptical about meditation because it used to be seen as only a religious practice end up converted when they give it a try. Don't immediately reject the idea before you have at least given it a try.

Need some more evidence? Well, in 2012, a survey conducted in the US involving 34,525 adults found that 1.9% of them had practiced mindfulness that year. Those that *had* meditated for general wellbeing and to prevent diseases (73%) and to reduce stress (92%). Some even meditated for better sleep and saw positive results.

It's proven to help with PTSD and trauma from childhood, chronic health conditions, and even mental illness. Other positive impacts can include:

- Focus: want to concentrate better? Studies have proven that mindfulness heals the neural pathways in your brain and helps you to focus better.

- Stress, anxiety, and depression: the calmness mindfulness brings to your body is immense and helps to untangle your thoughts, as discussed earlier in this book, which effectively improves your mood and ability to cope with things.

- Blood pressure: yep, that's right. A 2020 study found that regular mindfulness practice significantly reduces your blood pressure, which can help with diabetes, heart conditions, and kidney conditions, too.

- Pain: many studies have been conducted on the effects of mindfulness on chronic pain, and all of them have yielded positive results. This can also be helpful in other conditions where pain is a side effect, including cancer.

- Substance abuse: recovery from any addiction can be really hard. Mindfulness can assist people with cravings, triggers, and self-awareness, which is one of the hardest things to overcome in these hard times.

- Weight loss: again, finding triggers and self-awareness is very necessary when trying to lose weight, and studies have shown that mindfulness makes the journey so much easier.

- Attention-deficit hyperactivity disorder (ADHD): mindfulness can help calm down the brain, so it can be very helpful to people struggling with neurological disorders.

So now that you know the benefits of mindfulness, and you have tried some of the simple exercises, if you have started to see a difference, or if you want to explore further, try these everyday activities that can help to keep your attention on the present moment:

- Take mindfulness breaths: in between activities, take a second to press pause and just breathe. It will keep your brain from being tangled up in the last activity.

- Touch your chest and focus on your heartbeat. Notice it slow down as you calm.

- Be in nature: have a walk through the trees with your phone off so you can just exist where you are with mother nature, who will soothe you.

Mindfulness can work for anything and be tailored for your needs, as well. There are even trauma-informed mindfulness exercises which might be helpful for you, especially if you find yourself getting lost in your sadness and past every time you meditate. Please, take the time to explore this further if it's helpful for you, and here are some more simple exercises to try:

- Listen to your favorite song, carefully, noticing things

that you haven't picked up on before. Lyrics, instruments, sounds…

- Walk around your space and notice different textures. Touch things in the room to feel their hardness or softness, their roughness or smoothness. Notice it all.

- Go for a walk and count your steps. Try to focus on the steps and stop your mind from wandering—not easy, but more straight forward than sitting still with your eyes closed.

- Stretch. Notice how it feels in each of your muscles. See if there is any part of you that's tense or in pain.

- Take notice of all the colors around you. Which ones draw your attention? Which ones do you like best?

As you can see, these exercises don't take you deep into your mind to keep you in the present moment. You can also use your surroundings to keep yourself grounded. There are plenty of exercises like this which are under the umbrella of mindfulness but don't necessary include meditation. These might be more suitable for you. So, please, read on.

Here are some more tips for helping you to take control of your life to help you to recognize that you are the one with all the power:

- Identify your motivators and work out what's internal (your values and dreams) and external (such as social media pressures or pressures from your family). Work only on the ones that are yours.

- Create a vision for yourself: this can be something you do visibly, so you always have a reminder of what you're working towards. A vision board really works wonders!

- Don't let the negative thoughts take hold again. When they rear their ugly head, remind yourself that you *can* do it. Positive words of affirmation and separating yourself from the voice in your head can start you with this.

- Take personal responsibility for your life. Check in with yourself and make sure that you're being present where you need to be—only you can control that. Are you actively being there with your family? Are you eating and sleeping enough? Are you using your time and money wisely?

- Take note of the serenity prayer because it assists you in letting go of things you can't control: *God, grant me the serenity to accept the things I cannot change, courage to change the things I can, and wisdom to know the difference.*

- Process things before you respond, and don't immediately react because that's where you lose control of everything. This is where you need to learn to deal with your emotional triggers, as talked about in this chapter.

- Create a routine that helps you move in the right direction without being overwhelming. Small steps toward your goal are better than no steps at all.

- Rest: it's *very* important to know when to take breaks so you don't break yourself.

However, if none of this is good enough for you, and you feel like you need more, consider medical intervention. This can come in many forms. Medication may be one avenue, but you could also take a look at therapy.

Many therapists and professionals recommend specific types of therapy for people growing from trauma. These many or may not be right for you, but it's worth knowing what they are so you can do your own research.

EDMR

Eye Movement Desensitization and Reprocessing (EMDR) is a therapy that assists you in recovering from the emotions that come with trauma. Francine Shapiro, Ph.D., an American psychologist, developed the technique in the 1980s. She developed this when noticing that certain eye movements made it easier for her to think about her own trauma.

Studies came from this idea, and the tests that were run on many people helped to achieve EMDR's goal, which was to help you heal from trauma.

Patients often end up experiencing a number of things from this style of treatment, including:

- Desensitization: The thoughts are slowly combined with the eye movements to help the patient get used to the connection.

- Installation: The negative thoughts are eventually replaced with positive ones.

- Body Scan: This is looking at tension in the body when thinking about this trauma. What comes up? Where do you get tense?

- Closure: This involves discussions on how you feel now to see if the therapy has helped.

This style of therapy is often recommended for the following conditions, so if any of them have affected you, please look into your local services:

- Anxiety: from generalized to social anxiety, EMDR can help with all of it.

- Depression: whether this is severe or comes in episodes, EMDR will often be recommended.

- Dissociative conditions, such as dissociative identity disorder or amnesia can be helped.

- Eating disorders of all kinds can be helped with EMDR.

- Gender dysphoria can also be assisted.

- Obsessive-compulsive disorders.

- Personality disorders, such as the ones talked about earlier in this book, can be worked through with EMDR.

- Trauma disorders, such as PTSD, can also be helped with EMDR.

DBT

Dialectical behavior therapy (DBT) is often recommended for healing from emotionally immature parents. It looks at your behaviors and how they are affected by your emotions, especially if you struggle to regulate your emotions. DBT aims to help you:

- Understand your emotions and learn to accept them.

- Work out the most effective ways to manage these feelings.

- Figure out how to make positive changes to impact your life moving forward.

In this therapy, you will also learn how two opposite things can both be true, and you'll figure out ways to manage that. For example, you can love your parent but not always like how they behave. Since you can't control this behavior, all you can do is find ways to manage your reaction to it.

Talk Therapy

This can come in many different forms:

- Cognitive behavioral therapy (CBT): this teaches you ways to change your behavior, which will then, in turn, affect your mindset. This therapy comes with a lot of work to do at home to change your routines and lifestyle.

- Guided self-help: this involves working through a CBT workbook at home but with a therapist watching over your progress.

- Counselling: this involves talking to a trained professional and working through your feelings with them.

- Behavioral activation: this involves finding practical steps to start enjoying life again when you have experienced something difficult.

- Interpersonal therapy (IPT): this talks through and addresses issues in the relationships in your life and can focus on your parents if that's what you need.

- Mindfulness-based cognitive therapy (MBCT): this will help you focus on your thoughts and feelings in the present moment. This will often involve some of the mindfulness exercises and techniques we have previously discussed.

- Family therapy: this can help people who have difficult relationships with someone in their life and help you and your parent find better ways to communicate with one another.

You can even look out for self-help groups in your area because studies have shown that meeting other people who have been through similar situations in their lives can be hugely beneficial to you. Hearing ways to heal from medical specialists is one thing, but hearing it from peers who have tried and tested certain methods can be *really* great.

Not only do you get to hear similar stories and know that you aren't alone in your situation, but you will also find new friends who understand you in a way that no one else in your life does. You'll find a safe space where you belong (which, as discussed before, will assist you with your self-esteem).

Many people who have been to group therapy after suffering a childhood growing up with emotionally immature parents have found the following benefits:

- A reduction in symptoms and issues that have come from your childhood: anxiety, depression, PTSD, etc.

- It's more affordable than other types of therapy.

- It's a space where people can fully be themselves, trust themselves, and learn to trust other people, as well.

- It helps to shake off the stigma and shame, validating anything that people have suffered.

If this is something that sounds more like an option you would want to try, please take the time to look in your local area to see if there is anything there for you. You can also talk to your doctor to see if they know what's out there.

For more information about any of these types of therapy and the effects they can have on you, check out the CDC database of statistics about mental health help. There will also be a list of resources there if that's what you need, and you don't want to reach out to the medial professionals in this area.

But what do you specifically want to work on in therapy? What has been affected most of all? Chances are, you're struggling with your self-esteem because you have never really been validated in your life, so let's take a deeper look at that first to see if there is something you can do to help yourself live a happier, more fulfilled life, working toward those core values you have identified.

You *can* become the best version of yourself, and this book is here to help you with that. Before we dig much deeper into the impact this has all had on your self-esteem and what you can do to heal, let's take a pause to think about the best version of yourself and who you want to be:

- Visualize it: see who you want to become and keep that version of you in the forefront of your mind at all times. To help you with this, you can even write a letter to yourself, either one or ten years in the future, so you have accountability and a way to check in on yourself.

- Pick some goals that match your core values—small ones and ones that will take longer to give you something to focus on and get you to that future version of yourself you want to be.

- Stop the negativity, the criticism of yourself and others, people pleasing, procrastinating, and fear of failure.

You need to start to treat yourself with unconditional love, which might feel impossible right now, but the next chapter is going to help you with this. So, please, read on and start to find a better future just for you.

Chapter 7: Improving Self-Esteem

What do you see when you look in the mirror? Is it a version of yourself that you like? Or even one you can accept? Think about this really hard and take a good look. Don't just take a look at the physical. That's a part of this because, of course, how we perceive ourselves has an impact on us. But take a look deeper inside. Really see you.

You might try to compare yourself to others, but that's needless because you are not them. You are *you,* and everyone has something special about themselves. It might be hard to see that right now because you have grown up in an environment that didn't allow you to look inwards. You have always been focused on other people. But it's there, and as soon as you start doing the work on yourself, that will come to light.

You might see all the negative sides of yourself because that's what you have trained yourself to focus on. You might be tempted to beat yourself up because of mistakes or negative thinking. But, again, none of that is you. You know how to speak kindly to other people but not yourself. Knowing how to speak to yourself in the same manner is important.

Your self-esteem is actually made up for four components:

- Self-confidence: knowing that your basic needs are met is a great foundation to start building on. Without that, it's much harder to grow because, again, this leaves you in survival mode, just focused on trying to meet those basic needs. Reach out for help if you're struggling with this. Find someone who can help guide you because you *need* to get out of this existence mode so you can *live*. There *are* resources to assist you; you simply need to search for them.

- Identity: knowing who you are and what you believe in is also very important. Your body, your gender, sexuality, culture, beliefs, and even your job can contribute toward this. Take some time to work out who you are and what's important to you. If you have been stuck under someone else's shadow your whole life, you might not know who you are... but I promise you that you're in there somewhere. Dig deep enough, and you will start to accept *you*.

-

Belonging: a sense of belonging is extremely important, so having a place where you feel safe, such as within your family, your friendship group, or even your workplace, can help you know yourself fully. If you don't currently have a place where you feel like you belong, you need to seek it out, so you don't end up becoming lonelier and more isolated. Use your hobbies and interests to seek out groups of people who are just like you. Make some new friends and find a place where you can be yourself in this world.

- Confidence in your abilities will also bring you a sense of self-control—a sense of knowing who you are. Failures will happen, but that doesn't change what you're able to do. Don't focus on the negatives, and concentrate on the positives instead. Think about what you do well. Do you have a skill? Are you a great listener? Can you make people laugh with your singing? It doesn't need to be something massive. Small wins are still wins.

Have a think about all four aspects in your own life. Do you have them all under control? Is there anything listed here that you maybe need to work on? Take some time to study your reflection, thinking of all these aspects. Ask yourself how you can ensure that your basic needs are met. Take some time to work out your identity and who you are. Have a moment to consider where you belong, and also make note of things you're good at and what you like about yourself... keep this list with you to refer back to when needed.

Studies have actually gone on to show that the internal locus of control in the brain is actually directly linked to self-esteem. How well all the regions connect in our brain is how we see ourselves. It sounds scary but, again, is something that we can work on with exercises that we will go on to explore further in this chapter.

Self-esteem comes from how you feel about yourself and can be positive, negative, or a mix of both. The cause of these feelings can come from a number of different places, and here are main causes:

- Disapproval, particularly from the important people in your life, such as parents, teachers, or other authority figures.

- Parents with emotional immaturity, no matter what type of emotionally immature parent they are.

- Abuse in any form: mental, physical, or sexual.

- Walking on eggshells because of a bad relationship with your parents.

- Being bullied and having no help.

- Struggling with school and academia.

- Religious guilt and trauma.

- The patriarchal unattainable beauty standards we are faced with in the media and society every single day.

- Unrealistic perfectionism and goals, leaving you feeling like you never meet up.

Self-esteem isn't so much how we see ourselves; it's more how we value ourselves and how we assume we're perceived by others. It's different to self-image, which is more about appearances, and the effects of it run that much deeper.

So, as you can see, these are mostly external factors. We often put so much of our self-worth on the shoulders of those around us, allowing the outside world to affect us. It's very challenging not to be impacted by the outside world, and it's normal to do so, but when it gets to be too much, we can start to show the following symptoms:

- Self-doubt and fear.

- A constant cycle of shame, guilt, and humiliation.

- A constant stream of negative intrusive thoughts.

- An inability or refusal to take on any responsibility.

- Lack of boundaries.

- Withdrawal from the outside world and social events.

- A tendency to lash out emotionally.

- A real aversion to compliments which seems excessive.

- Health issues with no obvious cause: sleeplessness, headaches, stomach and back pain, constant exhaustion, no focus, etc.

This means that the negativity has become too much and is all-consuming. If this is allowed to continue for too long, it can lead to a number of mental health issues. Tackling this low self-esteem as early as you can is the best way to tackle it, especially when it comes from a lifetime of living with emotionally immature parents.

Here is some great advice when it comes to improving your self-esteem:

- Pick Out and Argue Back With Your Negative Beliefs: notice how they make you feel. It can also be helpful to challenge these beliefs when they rise up. I bet you can find some evidence to contradict yourself.

- Pick Out the Positives: make a note of the things you like about yourself, and maybe take note of compliments you get from other people. This can be referred back to whenever you're feeling particularly low.

- Build Positive Relationships and Avoid Negative Ones: notice the people in your life who aren't bringing positivity and slow the relationship with them. Anyone who brings you positivity is who you should focus on. They are the relationships that will continue to bring you joy in the future.

- Give Yourself a Break: perfection is unattainable, so don't keep chasing it. You also don't need to be cruel to yourself, especially when you have a bad day or a dip in your self-esteem. That will only create a vicious cycle and bring you lower.

- Choose Yourself and Learn to Say No: being a people pleaser doesn't make anyone happy. It leaves you overburdened and stressed out. Learning how to say "no" can be empowering and increase your self-belief.

- Improve Your Physical Health: focus on exercise because having a healthy body leads to a healthier mind. People with low self-esteem don't look after themselves as much as they should. They neglect their own needs in favor of others who they deem more important. Exercise, sleep, and a healthy diet will benefit you overall, including the way that you see yourself.

- Take On Challenges: learning something new, especially if you succeed, is guaranteed to make you feel better about yourself. Look at what you can do!

While trying to improve your self-esteem, it's important to focus on the small steps. It's taken a lifetime to get to where you are. That won't be undone overnight! Celebrate every tiny step, every little win, and keep reminding yourself that you're doing better than yesterday. Or even if you're not, you recognize that now, which is a plus—something you didn't know before.

If you think you might be suffering from depression or anxiety due to this low self-esteem, a medical professional can point you in the right direction. Talk therapy or medication might be right for you.

Here are some tips while you're waiting for your appointment:

- Get to know you: this information can be very useful when you speak to someone, but also for yourself. What do you find hard? What makes you happy? What triggers you? The more you know about yourself, the easier it is to live a happier life. The more you listen to your body and react to what it needs, the healthier a person you will be.

- Recognize when it's good: no matter how small these happy moments are, praise yourself and enjoy them. Try to focus more on them than the negative times. See your worth in these moments, especially if you have helped others.

- Build a support network: this doesn't just have to be medical professionals, but others in your life, as well. Having trusted friends or family members around can help you feel much less alone. These people can also pick you up when you are low.

- Take on challenges: if you aren't up for volunteering or learning something new, take your healing journey as your first challenge. Once you start on this, you'll find each success is easier to spot. If you hit on mistakes along the way, don't worry; that's all part of growth. Learning how to deal with these errors is just another lesson we all have to face at some point.

But one of the most important things you will need to do is heal from your past. Being stuck in what happened during your childhood means you can't ever move forward. There will always be a giant hurdle in your path, blocking you from your full potential.

Healing, with the help of a therapist or someone you trust, will open up doors you didn't even know were closed to you. Getting rid of that weight will allow you to become the person that you were always meant to be.

We have talked a lot about mindfulness in this book, and this can apply to your self-esteem, as well. Here are some exercises for you to try to see if this can assist you with your self-improvement:

Three Steps Inward

When choosing self-compassion, there are three ways you can do this:

1. Treat yourself with the same kindness and understanding you would a friend. You wouldn't call them stupid or useless for not understanding something right away, so don't speak to yourself like that either.

2. Remember that we all suffer. Humans go through bad times and also make mistakes. You're not alone in any of this.

3. You can be mindful of yourself, focus on your breathing and let the negative thoughts fly over you. Just because you think it doesn't mean it's true.

These are considered the three steps inward because engaging one will help you engage the others. They are all part of the positive cycle, which will hopefully replace the negative one you have been struggling with.

The Self-Care Break

Using a similar idea to the three steps inward, the self-care break is a way to physically stop and remind yourself that nothing is final and that you will be okay.

1. Press your hands to your heart and feel it beating. Focus on the beats and listen to them calmly.

2. Breathe deeply and focus on the air as it goes in through your nose and comes out through your mouth. Feel the air travel through your body.

3. Say to yourself the mantras from three steps inward:

- *This is just a moment.*

- *Everyone suffers; I am not alone in this.*

- *I deserve compassion in this moment.*

These phrases are to remind yourself to feel and accept the negative emotions as the come, but not to allow them to consume you. No one deserves that. You wouldn't want the same to happen to someone in your life. Imagine how horrible it would be to know someone you love is struggling with the same negativity.

Truth is, they probably are.

It might be great to reach out to those you trust in your life, as well, while you're doing the work and to offer some help to others. Nothing makes you feel better than seeing something you have done while assisting other people. Take them on the journey with you and give them a self-care break.

There are also many practical ways in which you can practice self-love, and here are some ideas to get you started:

- Make a Vision Board: this way, you can solidify your goals and see them all the time. It will serve as a constant reminder of the healing journey that you're on and where you want to be at the end of it.

- Learn About You: dig deep and discover more about who you are., You have spent years focused on everyone else, and you have gotten lost along the way. What sort of personality type are you? Do some tests to figure it out. What do you like to do? Explore new hobbies that you've never been brave enough to.

- Move Your Body: exercise is so important when it comes to self-love because it releases endorphins and improves your mood and overall wellbeing. This doesn't have to be a gym workout to start with; it can be yoga or a walk in the countryside, whatever you enjoy that gets you up and moving.

- Write Yourself a Love Letter: we often find ways to show thanks and appreciation to those around us but not to ourselves. Write yourself a letter and pick out your positive qualities and what you do well. Think about what you're proud of and what you enjoy doing. This letter will serve as a reminder when times get tough.

- Connect With Nature: fresh air is one of the quickest ways to clear our head, and sometimes, a walk is enough. But you can soon extend this to hikes and mountain climbs if you want, or even camping out in nature—whatever makes you smile.

- Take a Minute: meditation has cropped up a lot in this book, and for a good reason; it's a proven way to make you feel better. You won't see the positives of a clearer head and a happier mindset until you give it a try. Take a minute to start and work from there.

- Check Yourself: if you find yourself slipping back into bad habits, check yourself and have a little self-talk. Remind yourself that bad times don't make for a bad life. You are not a bad person just because you made a mistake. The voice of doom sitting in our head doesn't always need to win. Sometimes, you can tell that voice to shut the hell up already!

Again, mindfulness can be really helpful with this. The pathways in our brain connect better when we are mindful, which assists us in our self-esteem journey, as shown by scientific studies that have looked deeply into this.

It's been shown that starting with asking yourself the following questions can be a great way to identify whereabouts you are and what you can do to move forward. Try asking yourself these questions while looking in the mirror to really *see* yourself:

- What can you do or stop doing to help calm your emotions? Look back at the emotion regulation chapter to help you with this.

- Think of your core values, and ask yourself how your life will feel in one month or six months if you start heading toward your goals. Will things be better?

- Small steps make big changes, so consider some small steps that you can take today and this week to make you feel better about yourself.

- Do you have any hobbies or something that you're passionate about? If not, why not try and seek out something that makes you happy. If so, do you often make time for these passions? Try and fit them in to your schedule.

- When did you last feel confident in yourself? What were you doing at that moment? Is this something you can recreate now to boost yourself?

- What can you do to get to know yourself better? Building a stronger relationship with *you* will help you connect better with the other people in your lives.

- Are you facing any issues with your personal relationships? This can be within your family, friendship group, or work. Is there anything that can be done on your end to fix this? Can you get a third party involved to moderate things if possible?

- What activities can you bring into your day to make you smile more?

- What habits would you like to start including in your schedule? We have talked a lot about mindfulness in this book. Will that assist you in any way?

- How can you deepen your relationships with the important people in your life? Being more open and honest can help, as can taking personal accountability.

-

How can you spend more time with the positive influences in your life? Who uplifts you and makes you feel better? What is it they do to assist you?

- Is there something standing in the way of your happiness? How can you bridge the gap and get there?

- Do you need to look at your finances? If overspending is something that you worry about, maybe consider a budget planner. If spending less would make you feel better, it's worthwhile.

- If you picked up a new healthy habit, how would that impact your life—on a day-to-day basis, but in a month as well? Does it seem like it would help you get closer to happiness? Make a vision board or a list to keep you focused on this habit if you think it will bring you to a much better place.

Aside from the practical mindfulness exercises that we have already discussed in the previous chapter, which will definitely assist you with your new self-esteem goals, here are some other practical tips for you to try out:

- Strengths List: you *do* have strengths; everyone does. Write these down and make note of how they benefit you and your life. You can even note how it positively affects the lives of other people around you. Explore these strengths with an open heart, create a vision board for yourself, and remind yourself that you *are* worthwhile.

- Journal how you feel about yourself and use this to try to find triggers that might pop up along the way, sending you spiraling into negative thoughts. This might be situations or obstacles; it might even be people. Identifying these triggers can help you to remove yourself from them or, at the very least, respond to them better.

- Eat mindfully: I know that this might seem strange at first, but it's a very helpful activity to help live in the moment. Often because of our busy lives, we eat on the go, using food for sustenance and not taking note of what we eat. We barely even taste it and never feel fulfilled, which only leads to more mindless snacking. Take the time to chew thoughtfully, sit still while you eat, and notice the tastes and textures of your food. In that moment, you are *only* there to eat; that's your one and only job. So, concentrate on that. Focus only on food. Have gratitude for the food as you eat, as well.

- Mirror gaze mindfully: I know, there's been a lot of looking in the mirror this chapter, but that's probably not something you do a lot. If you suffer with low self-esteem, then it might even make you uncomfortable. But the first step in change is getting out of our comfort zone, so this is actually a good thing. This isn't just looking at yourself; it's seeing yourself, as well. These tips can help you with it:

- Find a quiet place to sit comfortably in the mirror, so you can focus only on you. Make sure you can easily make eye contact with yourself in the mirror for this exercise to be effective.

- Set a timer for five or ten minutes to just sit with yourself and get used to the person staring back at you.

- Close your eyes to begin with and take some deep, mindful breaths—deep inhalations and exhalations, concentrating on the way the air travels through your body. Keep doing this until your mind feels clearer.

- As your body starts to relax, allow your breaths to come more naturally. Focus on tense spots in your body and visualize that tension slowly dissolving with each breath.

- Open your eyes and look into the mirror. Pay attention to the rhythm of your breath. Does it feel or sound any different as you gaze into the mirror?

- Consider the message in your eyes. Is it critical or kind? If you focus on the things of yourself you don't like, then imagine that distain fading away with every breath.

  - What thoughts come to mind? Pay attention to them and your feelings, as well, but don't allow them to control you. Imagine the thoughts and feelings simply floating over your head, not touching any real part of you.

  - Hold your gaze for the time until the timer dings, allowing the thoughts to roll past you while offering yourself some kindness. Remember the nice things that people have said to you over the years and try saying them to yourself.

  - Once the time is over, take that sense of calm and self-acceptance with you. The more you mirror gaze, the more you will start to accept yourself.

- Practice self-compassion mindfully: studies have shown that you can use mindfulness to help yourself taper off the negative thoughts and replace them with positive ones. Being kind to yourself is massive when it comes to your self-esteem. There are thought to be three pillars of self-compassion, which you can use to tailor to your own needs:

- Replace self judgement with self-compassion. Try and change the story that you're telling yourself. Change the way you speak to yourself about everything. Don't focus on the one bad thing that happened today but the ten good.

- Humanity over isolation: this doesn't mean seek out company all the time because everything needs to happen in balance. You might *need* some time to yourself. Instead, this is referring to issues you are facing and the negative way you see yourself. You are never alone in anything you're going through. You aren't the only one who isn't perfect; no one is. The world would be boring if anyone was. You aren't the only person who doesn't like the way you look. That is common human suffering. Even those who are most outwardly confident have self-esteem issues. All humans suffer. Change the "I" to "we."

- Choose mindfulness: over-identifying is how we end up getting caught in that vicious cycle. Instead of getting caught up in our thoughts or feelings, label them in the way that we discussed earlier in this book, and distance yourself from them. That way, you can see things much more clearly.

Again, the best way I can put it is to speak to yourself in the same way that you would speak to a friend. Would you be so cruel to your best friend if she accidently sent an important email to the wrong person? Would you call your friend "ugly," "fat," and "useless?" No, you wouldn't, because then they wouldn't be your friend anymore. So why do you keep speaking to yourself like that? Try to change the words that you use with self-talk. Don't call yourself names, and instead focus on the positive things that you can do to improve situations.

A lot of the things discussed in this chapter will need a bit of a life overhaul to be effective, but if you didn't want the change, then you wouldn't be here. Starting a new, healthier habit and lifestyle can feel a little daunting, which is why the next chapter covers ways to help you with this. We will look at starting new habits and including healing techniques in our journey, leaving you with no excuses. No one is "too busy" to make their own lives better... and if they are, that is an issue that needs to be focused on in itself!

Take time for yourself because you are important, as well. I hope this book has taught you as much so far.

Chapter 8: Regular Reminders

So, working on the healing process is a long, personal journey which will cause you to go through stages. How these stages look is personalized, but it's a similar process for everyone. The steps will look a lot like this as you go:

- *Crisis* – this is the moment we hit rock bottom and can't take anymore. It's hard to lock into our rational thoughts because our emotions overwhelm us. It's likely you reached that stage with your emotionally immature parents just before picking up this book. While this is something we all experience, we can't get lost in these emotions and thoughts. They aren't helpful for anyone.

- *Equilibrium* – reaching a crisis has us wanting to escape from it to find some kind of normal. This often involves removing ourselves from a situation to give us time to calm down, i.e., taking yourself out of your parents' home after an argument. This can be a hard stage to reach, and it may even take some time, but you always get there.

- *Understanding* – once life has returned to normal a little, our brains can start to process and understand what's happened. You can use your history and previous experiences to identify why things went wrong... why the argument happened and got so explosive.

- *Awareness* – this is what we have been doing in this

book. Looking at the pattens of self-destructive behavior that you have participated in and acknowledging what is your parent's issue will give you some distance from the problems and allow you to look at things from various angles.

- *Confrontation* – this will start with the work on yourself, when you begin to confront yourself and the way you have been living. The obstacles in the way will feel easier to overcome once we examine them properly. For example, you might start to see how you escalated things and why your communication wasn't perfect.

- *Transcendence* – working through the trauma with the help of a therapist will allow you to uncover the real you. You will transcend into the better version of yourself. Yes, you might miss parts of your old life, especially if you have had to cut people off such as your parents, but eventually, an acceptance of a better future will come for you.

- *Incineration* – this is where rebirth happens. You have burned down your old life, so it's time to start again, to rebuild. You have confronted your demons and thrown everyone off your Mindful Bus who doesn't deserve to be there. It's scary but refreshing to aim for the life you visualize to yourself.

- *Liminality* – there will be dark times in your healing journey when it feels too hard or you aren't quite sure where to go, but these grey times are to be expected. Don't allow them to derail you or make you feel like none of this is worth it. There are always ways to keep you going, which this chapter will dive deeper into. The reminders will make sure you don't fall no matter what the hurdle is in your path.

- *Rebuilding* – now that you have started over and survived the grey times, you can focus on the path you want to take next. Where do you want to go? Who do you want to be? Remember your core values because they will help guide you to the best life you can have.

- *Arrival* – you can finally see the light at the end of the tunnel. Whatever path you have picked for yourself is finally working and starting to make you feel like a brand-new person. The weights that have been pressing down on you for your whole life have lifted, and you can finally be *you*—the you that you were always meant to be. Yes, there were years wasted because of the emotionally immature parents that you grew up with, but that doesn't mean *everything* is wasted. You still have many great years ahead of you to let yourself shine and be happy. You can focus on what makes you happy, what helps you self-actualize. Be creative, have fun, and make up for lost time.

No healing is a straightforward process, which is why regular reminders are vital. This will help to prevent us from slipping back into old, negative patterns of behavior. This isn't just something that will be done in a few weeks and then will never have to thought about again. It's a constant, ongoing process… but don't let that overwhelm you because often, when people start on their healing journey, they *want* to keep up the good habits they have learned along the way. Those little check-ins can make you feel much better.

Self-care reminders aren't just important for someone with childhood trauma and emotionally immature parents. This is really something that *everyone* should be doing. The following advice can be used by anyone but may be particularly useful for you:

- Stabilization – surviving can often mean withdrawing into ourselves to feel safe. Finding safe spaces outside of yourself can be really challenging, but once you *do*, these spaces (i.e., your home) or people can be great to refer back to when you're having a bad day or when you need to remind yourself of the new path you're on.

- Mourning – part of healing and recovering from the trauma can be grieving over your childhood and everything that you missed. This isn't a linear process, and you may revisit it. These reminders might not be pleasant, but recognizing these emotions and feeling them are a part of life. It's important here to remember what made you feel good before and try that again.

- Reconnection – finding your sense of sense again, or for the first time if you haven't ever been able to because of your childhood, can be an obstacle to moving on. This will be something that you need to keep reminding yourself to do over time. Set up weekly or monthly dates to meet with friends or family members, so you can remind yourself to keep connected to other people.

Along the way, you might find yourself hitting bumps in the road and struggling to overcome them. But a bad day doesn't have to be the be-all and end-all of everything. It's easy to have *all or nothing* thinking and to sink when a bad day comes, but here are some reminders or mantras to keep yourself positive when things are hard:

- Everyone has bad days – recovery is a rollercoaster, and there *will* be bad days along the way. But that isn't unusual. Everyone has bad days, everyone faces obstacles, and there's no need to have shame and guilt over this. These days are lessons more than something to send you spiraling backwards. Use these times to learn your best coping mechanisms and remind yourself of how far you've come.

- Temporary fixes are just that – it can be so easy to sink down into negative feelings when something does go wrong and go back to vices that have gotten us through before, such as alcohol. But these fixes haven't worked before, have they? There's a reason why you wanted to move away from that behavior, so don't forget that. Always keep that in mind and focus on the long-term end goal.

- Negativity doesn't define you –something going wrong doesn't define your whole recovery journey. Bad moments are just that: a little moment in time. Keep your eyes on the bigger picture.

- You are not alone – finding a support group or friends who understand your journey can be really useful. Having someone to contact when times are tough will often be a lifesaver along the way. This can be an online group or people you meet in person. Take a look at local support groups to help you remember that you aren't alone.

Try not to focus exclusively on the negatives you might come across on your healing journey. Here are some other tips to help you concentrate on the positives along the way:

- Every moment is brand new. You do not have to hold onto discomfort or a moment of negativity. Just concentrate on moving forward and the next moment.

- You are not a bad person because you are feeling discomfort. You're also not a bad person for having a slip-up. Remember, no one is perfect.

- A negative experience does not mean that you are being punished. It means you may be neglecting your intuition, well-being, and your personal truth. That's okay; you can easily get back on track.

- It's really okay to let go of the past. It means that you are giving yourself permission to be set free, and you need to be set free. Your emotionally immature parents have kept you in jail for a long time, but now, it's time to concentrate on you.

- You can find help. Help is out there. This can be friends, a support group, or even a medical professional. All you need to do is reach out and seek it.

- Ease up on yourself and allow your thoughts to flow

through you. They are only visitors; you don't have to set up a guest room for them. Thoughts don't always speak the truth, either. That's why you simply need to let them slide past you and go.

- Find something that calms your spirit and do it! When you do stuff that you love, you are putting space between you and discomfort. That leaves more room for you to feel renewed. Hobbies, exercise, or a moment in time... take it just for you.

- Create a mantra (a phrase that you believe with all your heart) and say it in the morning when you wake up and at night before you go to bed. *I am not my parents, my wellbeing is important, I am divine...* whatever works for you.

- Trust as you move away from the conditions that created the discomfort that you will be restored to your natural state of health and well-being. Trust the process and the healing journey. It will work for you.

- Allow yourself to feel the discomfort. Talk yourself through it and remind yourself that it's not going to last forever. Sometimes, when we struggle or resist things, they tend to get worse. Feel it and move on.

- Appreciate any moment of relief. Appreciation puts

you right in the flow of your natural state of being. If you hang around in appreciation long enough, that negative situation will not be able to hang around that much longer.

We can go even further to give you some recommendations to help you get through on a day-to-day basis. Sometimes, when we examine the bigger picture, which is something that we all must do, the small things are important, too:

- Set an intention and write it down. The intensions don't have to be massive; it can simply be "remain mindful around the kids," "smile at everyone you come across," or "focus on *me*," just something to take with you on a daily basis.

- Tell others your new intention and ask them to wish you well. Keep reminding yourself that this is your intention for the day so you can hold yourself accountable.

- Check in with this intention every so often. It might even be useful to keep saying it out loud. Put visual reminders everywhere, too, so you are always checking in.

- Use mindfulness to your advantage. Schedule five minutes in the morning, afternoon, and evening to rest and take note of everything happening with your body and breath. You can even use mindfulness apps and bells to keep yourself on track throughout the day.

- Review at the end of your day. Just take a moment to see how you did and how you feel. Good or bad, it doesn't matter; just concentrate on *you*.

Along the way, you *might* find negative emotions, especially during mindfulness, such as:

- Negative feelings, such as frustration or anger; this might be directed at yourself or other people in your life.

- High stress levels or maybe anxiety or fear, anything that puts you on edge.

- A deep sadness that affects every part of you.

- An unsettled feeling that borders on chaos and is hard to control.

- Negative thoughts about yourself.

- Distractions from your environment or within yourself.

- Intrusive thoughts and urges that leave you feeling very

guilty.

As long as you learn to work with these difficulties, they won't cause you as many issues as they might have before. Here are some tips to keep you on track:

- *Notice* and be mindful when these challenging thoughts and feelings crop up.

- *Notice* what your brain is telling you. Is it concocting a story to make you feel bad?

- *Notice* the physical sensations of the difficult emotion, such as stomach pain or a racing heart.

- Do the story and sensations change as you notice them? Give yourself some compassion because none of this is your fault. Find a way to be okay with these feelings.

- *Notice* the areas of resistance and the distractions flowing your way. Just don't allow them to take you away completely.

- *Notice* what is hard for you and where you forget to be mindful. Work out why this might be so it won't become a reoccurring issue.

None of these are easy emotions to feel and sensations to deal with, but you can do it. Mindfulness is just like any other habit. The more you practice it, the easier it will become to make it a part of your routine. If this is something you think you might struggle with, here is some science-based information that has proven tips to help you with this habit forming:

- Set a specific goal – write it down and make sure it's tangible. Not "I need to mediate more" but "I will meditate for fifteen minutes each day," something you can keep track of. Psych Net has presented a study that proves this works much better.

- Create a detailed, cue-based plan – you need to give yourself cues to remind you of your habit, such as mindfulness bells. Plenty of apps can assist you with this. There is a science behind this, as well, if you want to research further.

- Find a way to make it fun – sometimes our goals are hard to achieve because we don't enjoy them. You need to find a way to tempt yourself into being more mind-ful. Find activities you enjoy and do them mindfully. Pick perfect times that you will always want to do this. Studies show that tempting yourself means you keep up the habit.

-

Foster flexibility – don't be too rigid with yourself, or you will likely slip into old habits once more. Pubs Online suggests that if you are too hard on yourself, you will get frustrated and give up. If you missed mindfulness yesterday, then don't worry; carry on today. If you're late this morning, that's okay, too. Give yourself some credit.

- Socialize with it – creating habits with others makes us much more likely to stick to them. Evidence shows that once we have support or people to hold us accountable, we are more likely to stick to this.

It can also be really helpful to use the acronym for SMART goals to help keep your new, more positive habits intact. This can be great for reminding yourself of your new intentions along the way, too:

- **Specific** (simple, sensible, significant). This again refers to being careful with the wording for your goal, so it's something you can keep track of, e.g., *I want to socialize with my healthy family members regularly.*

- **Measurable** (meaningful, motivating). This is how you know you have achieved your goal, e.g., I want to socialize with my healthy family members *once a week.*

- **Achievable** (agreed, attainable). Make sure this is

Conclusion

S o, now you can see that the issues with your parents have never been *your* fault. You didn't do anything wrong; you weren't a "bad kid" or simply never good enough. You were just being *you,* or as much of yourself as you could be under their control. The emotional immaturity came with your parents; it isn't something you have done. You also can't change your parents; if they want to change, they need to do the work themselves.

The only person you can focus on is *you*.

So, how does that make you feel now? I bet you're feeling a very different way to how you were when you first started reading. I'm sure a weight has lifted off your chest, and you're feeling more positive about your future because the attention is finally on you. You're doing the work and making your own future so much brighter. How exciting is that?

Nucci, Larry (21 March 1981). "Conceptions of Personal Issues: A Domain Distinct from Moral or Societal Concepts". Child Development. 52 (1): 114–21. doi:10.2307/1129220. JSTOR 1129220.

Laupa, Marta (1 March 1995). "Children's reasoning about authority in home and school contexts". Social Development. 4 (1): 1–16. doi:10.1111/j.1467-9507.1995.tb00047.x.

Helwig, Charles C. (1 April 1998). "Children's Conceptions of Fair Government and Freedom of Speech". Child Development. 69 (2): 518–531. doi:10.1111/j.1467-8624.1998.tb06205.x. JSTOR 1132181.

Kim Ronald Hill; A. Magdalena Hurtado (1996). Aché Life History: The Ecology and Demography of a Foraging People. Transaction Publishers. ISBN 978-0-202-36406-3. Retrieved 15 June 2013.

Robert Alan LeVine; Barbara Bloom Lloyd (1966). Nyansongo: a Gusii community in Kenya. Wiley. Retrieved 15 June 2013.

Lancaster, Jane B; Lancaster, Chet S (1983). Ortner, Donald J. (ed.). "Parental Investment: Human Uniqueness Compared to "Great Apes": Likely Difference". How Humans Adapt: A Biocultural Odyssey. Washington: Smithsonian Institution. 967

495–525. doi:10.1146/annurev.clinpsy.121208.131208. PMC 3018741. PMID 20192797.

Stifter CA, Spinrad TL, Braungart-Rieker JM (1999). "Toward a developmental model of child compliance: the role of emotion regulation in infancy". Child Development. 70 (1): 21–32. doi:10.1111/1467-8624.00003. PMID 10191513.

Macklem, G.L. (2008). Practitioner's Guide to Emotion regulation in School–Aged Children. NY: Springer.[page needed]

Waller E, Scheidt CE (February 2006). "Somatoform disorders as disorders of affect regulation: a development perspective". International Review of Psychiatry. 18 (1): 13–24. doi:10.108 0/09540260500466774. PMID 16451876. S2CID 10215459.

Sim L, Zeman J (2006). "The contribution of emotion regulation to body dissatisfaction and disordered eating in early adolescent girls". Journal of Youth and Adolescence. 35 (2): 207–216. doi:10.1007/s10964-005-9003-8. S2CID 144601992.

Tice DM, Bratslavsky E, Baumeister RF (January 2001). "Emotional distress regulation takes precedence over impulse control: if you feel bad, do it!". Journal of Personality and Social Psychology. 80 (1): 53–67. doi:10.1037/0022-3514.80.1. 53. PMID 11195891.

ty". Frontiers in Human Neuroscience. 5: 17. doi:10.3389/fn hum.2011.00017. PMC 3039118. PMID 21347275.

Gary Deatherage (1975). "The clinical use of "mindfulness" meditation techniques in short-term psychotherapy" (PDF). Journal of Transpersonal Psychology. 7 (2): 133–43.

Karunamuni N, Weerasekera R (2019). "Theoretical Foundations to Guide Mindfulness Meditation: A Path to Wisdom". Current Psychology. 38 (3): 627–646. doi:10.1007/s12144-0 17-9631-7. S2CID 149024504.

Van Gordon W, Shonin E, Griffiths MD, Singh NN (2014). "There is Only One Mindfulness: Why Science and Buddhism Need to Work Together". Mindfulness. 6: 49–56. doi:10.100 7/s12671-014-0379-y.

Nisbet, Matthew (2017). "The Mindfulness Movement: How a Buddhist Practice Evolved into a Scientific Approach to Life". Skeptical Inquirer. 41 (3): 24–26. Archived from the original on 2018-10-02. Retrieved 2018-10-02.

Wilson 2014, p. 35.

"Sati". The Pali Text Society's Pali-English Dictionary. Digital Dictionaries of South Asia, University of Chicago. Archived from the original on 2012-12-12.

Dreyfus 2013, pp. 44–48.

102124. doi:10.1016/j.cpr.2022.102124. PMID 35078038. S2CID 245951867.

Black DS, Slavich GM (June 2016). "Mindfulness meditation and the immune system: a systematic review of randomized controlled trials". Annals of the New York Academy of Sciences. 1373 (1): 13–24. Bibcode:2016NYASA1373...13B. doi:10.11 11/nyas.12998. PMC 4940234. PMID 26799456.

Creswell JD, Lindsay EK, Villalba DK, Chin B (April 2019). "Mindfulness Training and Physical Health: Mechanisms and Outcomes". Psychosomatic Medicine. 81 (3): 224–232. d oi:10.1097/PSY.0000000000000675. PMC 6613793. PMID 30806634.

Liu YZ, Wang YX, Jiang CL (2017). "Inflammation: The Common Pathway of Stress-Related Diseases". Frontiers in Human Neuroscience. 11 (316): 316. doi:10.3389/fnhum.2017.0031 6. PMC 5476783. PMID 28676747.

Kelly SJ, Ismail M (March 2015). "Stress and type 2 diabetes: a review of how stress contributes to the development of type 2 diabetes". Annual Review of Public Health. 36: 441–462. doi:10.1146/annurev-publhealth-031914-1229 21. PMID 25581145.

Scott-Sheldon LA, Gathright EC, Donahue ML, Balletto B, Feulner MM, DeCosta J, et al. (January 2020). "Mindful-

something you can physically achieve; otherwise, you're likely to give it up way too easily, e.g., I want to socialize with my healthy family members *once a month*.

- **Relevant** (reasonable, realistic and resourced, results-based). Make sure you know why you want to do this, or you might let it slide before it can become established as a proper habit, e.g., I want to socialize with my healthy family members once a month, *so I can catch up with them and feel good about myself.*

- **Time bound** (a schedule for this to be done by or a time to check in). If you keep up this habit for six months, it will be more settled inside of you. More than that, it's good to check in with how you're feeling in six months' time to ensure the goal is still working out for you.

There is a study which shows that you can actually form a habit in twenty-one days. This is less than a month, which isn't an overwhelming amount of time. If you can commit twenty-one days to help your recovery, you will be better for it.

During these twenty-one days, you will go through these stages:

Phase 1: The Honeymoon

During the beginning of this habit forming, your motivation and enthusiasm will be high, and the habit will be a novelty, so it will feel easy. Enjoy this time and the sensations that come with it because it doesn't last forever! The joy will subside because making a change in life is hard.

Phase 2: The Fight Through

The novelty wears off, and real life starts to get in the way. This is a really hard time to keep things going, which is why you need to fight through. There are certain ways you can force yourself to keep going through this slump:

- Recognition: see how you're feeling and recognize that this is an important time in the process. Taking note of how you feel will help you to keep going.

- Check in with yourself: remember why you're doing this and what the positive outcomes will be at the end. Maybe add some mini rewards to keep yourself going in the right direction.

- Life Projection: Envision what life will look like if you keep this up and have done a lot of work on yourself and your happier future. Keep referring back to this when times are tough. Keep fighting through.

Phase 3: Second Nature

Let this habit slowly become part of your everyday routine. The more you keep integrating it, the longer you will keep going, and you will finally see what all the hard work was for. It was worth it, honest! You're on your way to achieving that life projection you saw for yourself.

The slump will be the hardest time, so make sure you have a lot of support along the way to assist you with this. A lot of resources believe that this rollercoaster will happen over a period of about twenty-one days, with each day looking like the following:

- Days one to three – your habit is your favorite thing, and you are firmly in the honeymoon stage. Embrace every moment about this and keep note of how it makes you feel to get you through the slump. See what rewards work and what makes you a little doubtful. Use this to help you moving forward.

- Days four to ten – this is the slump, which you need to fight through. Most people who don't form a habit successfully lose faith and quit at this point. A week might not seem like a long time, but it's forever when something is hard. Have a support system to assist you with this. Have people to help you get through and remember all the things that felt good about the habit.

-

Days elven to fourteen – you might be on the other end of the slump, but you still have to keep focused. Don't let yourself slide or start to feel negative. Do whatever it takes to keep yourself motivated.

- Days fifteen to twenty – start a countdown towards the end of the twenty-one days to show how far you've come. Sit back and tale stock at the differences you have made in such a short space of time.

- Day twenty-one and beyond – the habit will be a part of your routine now, but that doesn't mean you shouldn't check in every so often to make sure you're still feeling good and that the habit is a healthy one.

But don't worry if you take less or more time to form the habit. There's no way to make this for each and every individual because we're all different and have unique needs. This is just a guide to get you started along the way.

The twenty-one days will of course be your main focus for this exercise, but you might need some reminders after, which is what this chapter is all about. So, here are some tips on what will help the habit stick around long term:

- Time – this is common for most people because our days typically revolve around time. Set reminders on your phone or set your new habit before you eat...

anything to fit it in around what you do every single day anyway. That way, you'll be less likely to forget.

- Location – the environment around us often triggers mindless automatic behavior. Assigning your new habit to a particular location (e.g., find a mindful spot) will help bring the behavior into your everyday life.

- Combine it with other habits – something you do every single day at certain times, such as eating, will help bring this new habit into your life. The trigger is already there.

- Emotions – bad habits often come with negative emotions (such as boredom eating or angry alcohol drinking). You might not find it as easy to connect your new habit to positive emotions, but you can *notice* when these negative emotions creep up and focus on your new habit instead.

- People – others can help you with your new habit. You can even go to local mindfulness classes to get you started.

There are also some great ways to keep yourself motivated, especially when you aren't feeling it. Here are some tips to keep on fighting if it's on day four or forty-four:

- Keep setting goals – focus on the final achievement but keep setting goals along the way.

- Surround yourself with the right people – toxic and negative people won't serve you well. There isn't any reason to keep them around.

- Use your vision board or some other visual reminder to keep you going even through your darkest days.

- Keep having fun – if things become boring, we're more likely to drop them and allow our distractions to get the better of us.

- Have someone tell you off – if this works for you, have someone you trust hold you accountable for when you aren't doing what you're supposed to be.

- Smaller steps – if things become overwhelming, that's okay; just break things down into smaller, more manageable steps to keep you going.

- Treat yourself – whenever you do something good, have a reward—a sweet treat or a coffee with friends, or whatever works best for you.

- Embrace the mornings – successful people *love* the mornings. I don't, but I have to admit that I do always feel better when I get up earlier and have some time to just *be* before the hectic nature of everyday life gets the better of me. This is a great time to reflect and to examine where I am right now.

- Stay healthy – it's hard to keep up with anything when we aren't eating right or exercising enough, and if we don't sleep well... forget it! For these twenty-one days (or however long it takes), you have to prioritize you!

- Reframe your setbacks – so, you didn't meditate all day because you were stuck in meetings. This doesn't mean you should give up or start over. Meditate before bedtime instead. Or use it as a lesson to see how different you feel today instead of the days you have been meditating. We can always learn and grow.

- Visualize where you want to be – and, finally, keep your end goal in mind always because that's where you're headed, after all. Keep your eyes on the prize.

Phew, what a rollercoaster, but we've finally made it to the end... of the book anyway, but this is only the start of your healing journey. But before you go, I want to share some parting words with you, so we can check in to see if we're in the same place we were at the start of the book.

Read on; you might surprise yourself. Even if you haven't started the work yet, I bet you're already starting to look at things a little bit differently.

Part 4 - Some Parting Words

Noting the effect that your emotionally immature parents had on you as a child and as an adult, such as the guilt and shame you have likely carried with you through life, will help you to recover from these effects. They can help you build good habits and keep on moving forward.

You *can* heal, and you will if you work on yourself. There might be some times when it's hard, but as we've discussed through this book, you can keep yourself going and get yourself through it. Nothing needs to stand in your way.

Whatever type of emotionally immature parent yours is, this book has shown you ways in which you can move forward:

Emotional Parents

You've lived in the shadows of someone else's feelings for far too long. Now it's time to start focusing on your feelings and your triggers. It's time to look inwards and know what makes you happy. It's not easy to do when you've spent so long worrying about others, but it's time. You've spent too long looking outwards. Now look in.

Driven Parents

Your parents have always been highly invested... *too* invested at times, bordering on controlling. Setting strict boundaries with these parents will be challenging, but you need to start creating a decent space for yourself so you can heal. Make sure you revisit these boundaries all the time to ensure they still suit you. Tighten or loosen them as you need to.

Passive Parents

You have always had your problems lessened and minimized because your parent didn't like to face anything awkward and uncomfortable. To try to improve your relationship with this parent, you will need to communicate very clearly and make sure your needs are explained and hopefully understood by the other person.

Rejecting Parents

If your parent has always wanted to be left alone, the only way you can really treat them is with empathy. If it's too much for you that you will unlikely ever get anything back—unless they work on healing their own trauma—then it's time to limit your contact. It's time for you to be in control and set the limits you want. Focus on you. Don't reject yourself.

Your healing will be a journey, one that's likely to be a roller-coaster, so get as many people as you can on board to assist you with this. Focus on your friends, your healthy family members, and your support groups, as well. Create a positive circle around you—people who lift you up and make you feel better, who help you on the path toward your core values. This isn't something that you are alone in; you just need to reach out to get this help: medical or support system. Whatever works best for you.

If you think your needs are more serious, *please* look into your local resources or even contact a medical professional: a doctor or a therapist who can examine your individual situation and give you the right path. Everyone is different, and every healing path is individualized. Getting the perspective of an outsider and a professional can be really helpful for everyone.

In the introduction, I talked about the five steps of healing. Here, I will remind you of these, and I hope you feel like you're further along on your journey:

Step One: Know what's wrong.

I'm sure you are now more clued in to exactly what's wrong with you and your parents, too. You might have known that you had a lot of emotional immaturity in your life, but this book has clarified exactly what you went through. Knowing this will help you moving forward. Knowledge is power.

Step Two: Work on YOU!

I have shown you over and over that you can't fix someone who doesn't want to be helped, and even if they do want help, that isn't your responsibility. You have spent way too much of your life focused on other people, so now it's time to look at *you.*

Talk therapy or other therapy techniques can help you learn more about yourself. These people are experts and emotionally separated from the situation, so they can show you things you didn't even know yourself.

Step Three: Time to Connect

Connect with yourself first and foremost. Notice your own feelings, notice the sensations careering through your body, and work out what triggers you and makes you feel good or bad. Connect with you first and foremost so you know what you need. Once you know what you need, you can start reaching out once more.

Step Four: Meaningful Relationships

Now it's time to reach out and build decent relationships with other people. This can be connecting more with your friends and nontoxic family members. This can even be your parents. As long as you keep putting yourself first, this will be a positive part of your journey. Keep the positive relationships going and step back on the negative ones. Work out who brings something to your life and get rid of the people who only take things away. You no longer need that in your life. Find your place where you belong. Use that to keep yourself happy.

Step Five: Continue Healing

Continue healing all the time, long after you have finished reading this book. Use the tips in the previous chapters about mindfulness and forming new habits to make yourself a better person. A happier person. A healthier person, as well. Isn't that what we all want? Remember, your core values are vital to this. We have talked about this a lot because it's so important to know who you are and what's important to you. It can also assist you in keeping yourself on the right path no matter what happens.

I hope the research that has been put into this book has helped you open your mind to yourself and the people around you. I'm sure this has put you on the right path, but now it's time for you to work. Use the enthusiasm this book has given you to keep on moving forward. Good luck with the rest of your journey and concentrate on what makes you happy. Remember, reach out for help if you need it. Never feel like you're on your own. Someone is always out there to help you.

Please also heed the advice to try mindfulness because the benefits will really help you. Escaping the vicious cycle of thoughts, feelings, and behaviors will make you see the world differently. Not just with your parents but with you, too. You might even realize that you really *do* need the help, and more than you originally thought.

To seek out mental health help, check out the database of outlets compiled by MHA National or ADAA which will tell you where to look in your local area and the locations of all the specialist treatment centers. But if you can't find anything there, then your local doctor will be able to point you in the right direction.

If you want to know more about the scientific studies done in this area, NIMH has a lot of the studies and results presented to get you started, as does the Data Catalog.

The more you know, the more you can help yourself, and the better your future will be! As I said before, knowledge is power. The more you know about yourself, the more you can regain power and control over your life. The more you can be *you*.

Bibliography

Adult Children of Emotionally Immature Parents: How to Heal from Distant, Rejecting, or Self-Involved Parents by Lindsay C. Gibson

Handbook of Emotion Regulation by James Gross

Wechsler, David (1 March 1950). "Intellectual Development and Psychological Maturity". Child Development. 21 (1): 45–50. doi:10.2307/1126418. JSTOR 1126418. PMID 15420813.

"integration". APA Dictionary of Psychology. Retrieved 2022-01-14.

Adler, Nancy (November 1997). "Purpose in Life". Psychosocial workgroup. MacArthur. Archived from the original on 2022-01-13. Retrieved 2011-11-03.

University, Johns Hopkins (1885). "Circulars". 4. The Ohio State University: 106.

Bruner, Jerome S. (1 January 1972). "Nature and uses of immaturity". American Psychologist. 27 (8): 687–708. doi:10.1037/h0033144.

Bjorklund, DF (September 1997). "The role of immaturity in human development". Psychological Bulletin. 122 (2): 153–69. CiteSeerX 10.1.1.453.8039. doi:10.1037/0033-2909.122.2.153. PMID 9283298.

Yaremko, John, Mary A (2005). "2005 John and Mary A. Yaremko Programme on Multiculturalism and Human Rights Symposium Equality and the Family". Equality and the Family: 93.

Johnson Ph. D, M.P.H, M.D., Ph.D, Giedd, M.D, Sara B, Robert W, Jay N. (2009). "Adolescent Maturity and the Brain: The Promise and Pitfalls of Neuroscience Research in Adolescent Health Policy". Journal of Adolescent Health. 45 (3): 216–221. doi:10.1016/j.jadohealth.2009.05.016. PMC 2892678. PMID 19699416.

Erik H. Erikson (1968). Identity: Youth and Crisis. W. W. Norton. ISBN 978-0-393-31144-0. Retrieved 9 June 2013.

Kemph, John P. (1 March 1969). "Erik H. Erikson. Identity, youth and crisis. New York: W. W. Norton Company, 1968". Behavioral Science. 14 (2): 154–159. doi:10.1002/bs.383014 0209.

J. Eugene Wright (1 October 1982). Erikson, identity and religion. Seabury Press. ISBN 978-0-8164-2362-0. Retrieved 9 June 2013.

Francis L. Gross (1 February 1987). Introducing Erik Erikson: an invitation to his thinking. University Press of America. ISBN 978-0-8191-5789-8. Retrieved 9 June 2013.

Roweton, William E. (1 April 1988). "Gross, F. L., Jr. (1987). Introducing Erik Erikson: An invitation to his thinking. Lanham, MD: University Press of America. 148 pp., $23.50 (hard cover), $10.75 (paper)". Psychology in the Schools. 25 (2): 209–210. doi:10.1002/1520-6807(198804)25:2<209::AID-P ITS2310250218>3.0.CO;2-B.

Herbert Ginsburg; Sylvia Opper (1988). Piaget's Theory of Intellectual Development. Prentice-Hall. ISBN 978-0-13-675166-3. Retrieved 9 June 2013.

(2): 33–66Proceedings of the Seventh International Smithsonian Symposium

Johnson, Sara B.; Blum, Robert W.; Giedd, Jay N. (31 August 2009). "Adolescent Maturity and the Brain: The Promise and Pitfalls of Neuroscience Research in Adolescent Health Policy". Journal of Adolescent Health. 45 (3): 216–221. doi:10.1016/j.jadohealth.2009.05.016. PMC 2892678. PMID 19699416nihms:207310

Luna, Beatriz; Thulborn, Keith R.; Munoz, Douglas P.; Merriam, Elisha P.; Garver, Krista E.; Minshew, Nancy J.; Keshavan, Matcheri S.; Genovese, Christopher R.; Eddy, William F.; Sweeney, John A. (30 April 2001). "Maturation of Widely Distributed Brain Function Subserves Cognitive Development". NeuroImage. 13 (5): 786–793. CiteSeerX 10.1.1.330.7349. doi:10.1006/nimg.2000.0743. PMID 11304075. S2CID 754405.

Baird, Abigail A; Fugelsang, Jonathan A; Bennett, Craig M (April 2005). "What were you thinking?: An fMRI study of adolescent decision making" (PDF). Poster Presented at the Annual Meeting of the Cognitive Neuroscience Society, New York.

Steinberg, Laurence (1 April 2007). "Risk Taking in Adolescence: New Perspectives From Brain and Behavioral Science". Current Directions in Psychological Science. 16 (2): 55–59. doi:10.1111/j.1467-8721.2007.00475.x. S2CID 18601508.

McClure, Samuel M.; Laibson, David I.; Loewenstein, George; Cohen, Jonathan D. (October 15, 2004). "Separate Neural Systems Value Immediate and Delayed Monetary Rewards" (PDF). Science. New Series. 306 (5695): 503–507. Bibcode:2004Sci...306..503M. doi:10.1126/science.1100907. PMID 15486304. S2CID 14663380. Retrieved 15 June 2013.

Banich, Marie T. (2018). Cognitive neuroscience. Rebecca J. Compton (Fourth ed.). Cambridge, United Kingdom. ISBN 978-1-107-15844-3. OCLC 985974469.

Putnam, Robert D. (1 December 1995). "Tuning In, Tuning Out: The Strange Disappearance of Social Capital in America". PS: Political Science and Politics. 28 (4): 664–683. doi:10.2307/420517. JSTOR 420517. S2CID 14610751.

Buckingham, (1999). Oxford Review of Education, Political Education, 25, (1-2), pp. 171-184.

Eliasoph, Nina (31 July 1990). "Political culture and the presentation of a political self". Theory and Society. 19 (4): 465–494. doi:10.1007/BF00137622. JSTOR 657799. S2CID 140441785.

William A. Gamson (28 August 1992). Talking Politics. Cambridge University Press. ISBN 978-0-521-43679-3. Retrieved 15 June 2013.

Gallatin, Judith; Adelson, Joseph (1 April 1971). "Legal Guarantees of Individual Freedom: A Cross-National Study of the Development of Political Thought". Journal of Social Issues. 27 (2): 93–108. doi:10.1111/j.1540-4560.1971.tb00655.x.

Helwig, Charles C. (1 December 1997). "The Role of Agent and Social Context in Judgments of Freedom of Speech and Religion". Child Development. 68 (3): 484–495. doi:10.1111/j.1467-8624.1997.tb01953.x. JSTOR 1131673. PMID 29106706.

Ortiz, Adam (Jan 2004). "Cruel and Unusual Punishment: The Juvenile Death Penalty: Adolescence, Brain Development and Legal Culpability". Juvenile Justice Center, American Bar Association. Retrieved 15 June 2013.

Dena Taylor (1988). Red Flower: Rethinking Menstruation. Crossing Press. ISBN 978-0-89594-312-5. Retrieved 15 June 2013.

Janice DeLaney (1 January 1988). The Curse: A Cultural History of Menstruation. University of Illinois Press. ISBN 978-0-252-01452-9. Retrieved 15 June 2013.

Sheldon, K. M.; T. Kasser (2001). "Getting Older, Getting Better? Personal Strivings and Psychological Maturity Across the Life Span". Developmental Psychology. 37 (4): 491–501. doi:10.1037/0012-1649.37.4.491. PMID 11444485.

Franz, Warren, Watson, Angell, Shepherd I, Howard C, John B, James R. (1919). "Psychological Bulletin, Volume 16". Psychological Bulletin. American Psychological Association. 16: 312.

Mack, J. W. (1909). "The Juvenile Court". Harvard Law Review. 23 (2): 104–122. doi:10.2307/1325042. JSTOR 1325042.

J.E, M, Evans, Castle (1918). "The relation of mental age to chronological age as determined by certain individual and group tests". Journal of Applied Psychology. 2 (4): 308–322. doi:10.1037/h0074678.

Steinberg, Laurence; Elizabeth Cauffman (June 1996). "Maturity of Judgment in Adolescence: Psychosocial Factors in Adolescent Decision Making". Law and Human Behavior. 20 (3): 249–272. doi:10.1007/BF01499023. ISSN 0147-7307. JSTOR 1393975. S2CID 8733431.

"Personality disorders". medicineworld.org. Retrieved November 26, 2020.

Department of Veterans Affairs Regional Office in Winston-Salem, NC, Docket No 04-12 158A

Almeida, Fernando; Ribeiro, Patrícia; Moreira, Diana (September 27, 2019). "Immature Personality Disorder: Contribution to the Definition of this Personality" (PDF). Clinical Neuroscience and Neurological Research International Journal. Troy, Michigan: Academic Strive. 2 (2).

Ostrow, Ruth (May 18, 2017). "Forever young: immature personality disorder". The Australian. Retrieved December 28, 2020.

"2009 ICD-9-CM Diagnosis Code 301.89 : Other personality disorders". www.icd9data.com.

Pedersen, Liselotte; Simonsen, Erik (November 17, 2014). "Incidence and prevalence rates of personality disorders in Denmark—A register study". Nordic Journal of Psychiatry. Abingdon, England: Taylor & Francis. 68 (8): 543–548. doi:10.3109/08039488.2014.884630. ISSN 0803-9488. PMID 24520919. S2CID 207472992.

Krishnaram, Vaithiyam Devendran; Aravind, Vaithiyam Krishnaram; Vimala, A. Rupavathy (March 2016). "Deliberate Self-harm seen in a Government Licensed Private Psychiatric Hospital and Institute". Indian Journal of Psychological Medicine. Thousand Oaks, California: SAGE Publishing. 38 (2): 137–141. doi:10.4103/0253-7176.178808. PMC 4820553. PMID 27114626.

"Personality disorders :From MedicineWorld.Org". medicine world.org.

Diagnostic and Statistical Manual of Mental Disorders. American Psychiatric Association. 1952. p. 98,36.

Diagnostic and Statistical Manual of Mental Disorders, Second Edition. American Psychiatric Association. 1968. p. 44.

Diagnostic and Statistical Manual of Mental Disorders, Third Edition. American Psychiatric Association. 1980. p. 330. Other Personality Disorder should be used when the clinician judges that a specific Personality Disorder not included in this classification is appropriate, such as Masochistic, Impulsive, or Immature Personality Disorder. In such instances the clinician should record the specific Other personality Disorder, using the 301.89 code.

"International Classification of Diseases, Revision 6". 1948.

"International Classification of Diseases, Revision 7". 1955.

"Conversion Tables between ICD-8, ICD-9, ICD-10" (PDF). 1994. p. 14.

Severino, Sally K.; Mcnutt, Edith R. (March 1984). "The Psychiatrist as Expert Witness: The Roman Catholic Church Marriage Tribunal". Journal of the American Academy of Psychiatry and the Law. Bloomfield, Illinois: American Academy of Psychiatry and the Law. 12 (1): 49–66. doi:10.1177/0093185 38401200106. S2CID 158806167.

Kok, Lee Peng; Cheang, Molly; Chee, Kuan Tsee (1990). Diminished Responsibility: With Special Reference to Singapore. Kent Ridge, Singapore: NUS Press. pp. 157–158. ISBN 9789971691387.

"Decision order" (PDF). werc.wi.gov. 1989. Retrieved November 26, 2020.

Carney, Terry (2003). "Disability and Social Security: Compatible or Not?". Australian Journal of Human Rights. Abingdon, England: Taylor & Francis. 9 (2): 139–172. doi:10.1080/1323238X.2003.11911110. S2CID 158299198.

Dierickx, Sigrid; Deliens, Luc; Cohen, Joachim; Chambaere, Kenneth (December 2017). "Euthanasia for people with psychiatric disorders or dementia in Belgium: analysis of officially reported cases". BMC Psychiatry. London, England: BioMed Central. 17 (1): 203. doi:10.1186/s12888-017-1369-0. ISSN 1471-244X. PMC 5481967. PMID 28641576. S2CID 3237745.

Austin and Highnet, 2017[full citation needed]

Schechter DS, Willheim E (July 2009). "Disturbances of attachment and parental psychopathology in early childhood". Child and Adolescent Psychiatric Clinics of North America. 18 (3): 665–86. doi:10.1016/j.chc.2009.03.001. PMC 2690512. PMID 19486844.

Retz W, Stieglitz RD, Corbisiero S, Retz-Junginger P, Rösler M (October 2012). "Emotional dysregulation in adult ADHD: What is the empirical evidence?". Expert Review of Neurotherapeutics. 12 (10): 1241–51. doi:10.1586/ern.12.109. PMID 23082740. S2CID 207221320.

Pynoos RS, Steinberg AM, Piacentini JC (December 1999). "A developmental psychopathology model of childhood traumatic stress and intersection with anxiety disorders". Biological Psychiatry. 46 (11): 1542–54. CiteSeerX 10.1.1.456.8902. doi:10.1016/s0006-3223(99)00262-0. PMID 10599482. S2CID 205870651.

Schore, A., (2003). Affect dysregulation and disorders of the self. New York: Norton.[page needed]

Bjorkquist OA, Fryer SL, Reiss AL, Mattson SN, Riley EP (February 2010). "Cingulate gyrus morphology in children and adolescents with fetal alcohol spectrum disorders". Psychiatry Research. 181 (2): 101–7. doi:10.1016/j.pscychresns.2009.10.004. PMC 2815126. PMID 20080394.

Brewin CR, Cloitre M, Hyland P, Shevlin M, Maercker A, Bryant RA, et al. (December 2017). "A review of current evidence regarding the ICD-11 proposals for diagnosing PTSD and complex PTSD" (PDF). Clinical Psychology Review. 58: 1–15. doi:10.1016/j.cpr.2017.09.001. PMID 29029837. S2CID 4874961.

Clinical trial number NCT00467038 for "Treatment of Aggression, Anger and Emotional Dysregulation in Borderline Personality Disorder" at ClinicalTrials.gov

Dialetical Living. "What is Emotion Dysregulation?". www.dialecticalliving.ca/. Dialetical Living. Retrieved 1 April 2021.

De Caluwé E, Decuyper M, De Clercq B (July 2013). "The child behavior checklist dysregulation profile predicts adolescent DSM-5 pathological personality traits 4 years later". European Child & Adolescent Psychiatry. 22 (7): 401–11. doi:10.1007/s00787-013-0379-9. PMID 23381573. S2CID 24423401.

Barkley RA (January 1997). "Behavioral inhibition, sustained attention, and executive functions: constructing a unifying theory of ADHD". Psychological Bulletin. 121 (1): 65–94. doi:10.1037/0033-2909.121.1.65. PMID 9000892.

Stifter CA, Jain A (May 1996). "Psychophysiological correlates of infant temperament: stability of behavior and autonomic patterning from 5 to 18 months". Developmental Psychobiology. 29 (4): 379–91. CiteSeerX 10.1.1.590.8991. doi:10.1002/(sici)1098-2302(199605)29:4<379::aid-dev5>3.0.co;2-n. PMID 8732809.

Eisenberg N, Spinrad TL, Eggum ND (March 2010). "Emotion-related self-regulation and its relation to children's maladjustment". Annual Review of Clinical Psychology. 6 (1):

Kanske P, Schönfelder S, Forneck J, Wessa M (January 2015). "Impaired regulation of emotion: neural correlates of reappraisal and distraction in bipolar disorder and unaffected relatives". Translational Psychiatry. 5 (1): e497. doi:10.1038/tp.2014.137. PMC 4312831. PMID 25603413.

Heissler J, Kanske P, Schönfelder S, Wessa M (January 2014). "Inefficiency of emotion regulation as vulnerability marker for bipolar disorder: evidence from healthy individuals with hypomanic personality". Journal of Affective Disorders. 152–154: 83–90. doi:10.1016/j.jad.2013.05.001. PMID 23948633.

Calkins SD, Dedmon SE (April 2000). "Physiological and behavioral regulation in two-year-old children with aggressive/destructive behavior problems". Journal of Abnormal Child Psychology. 28 (2): 103–18. doi:10.1023/A:1005112912906. PMID 10834764. S2CID 18490690.

Garcia-Coll C, Kagan J, Reznick J (1984). "Behavioral inhibition in young children". Child Development. 55: 505–529.

Bronson M. B. (2000). Self-regulation in early childhood. New York: Guilford Press.[page needed]

Vilhena-Churchill N, Goldstein AL (May 2014). "Child maltreatment and marijuana problems in young adults: examining the role of motives and emotion dysregulation". Child Abuse

& Neglect. 38 (5): 962–72. doi:10.1016/j.chiabu.2013.10.009. PMID 24268374.

Kliewer W, Riley T, Zaharakis N, Borre A, Drazdowski TK, Jäggi L (September 2016). "Emotion dysregulation, anticipatory cortisol, and substance use in urban adolescents". Personality and Individual Differences. 99: 200–205. doi:10.1016/j.paid.2016.05.011. PMC 5082236. PMID 27795602.

Prosek EA, Giordano AL, Woehler ES, Price E, McCullough R (September 2018). "Differences in Emotion Dysregulation and Symptoms of Depression and Anxiety among Illicit Substance Users and Nonusers". Substance Use & Misuse. 53 (11): 1915–1918. doi:10.1080/10826084.2018.1436563. PMID 29465278. S2CID 3411848.

"Borderline personality disorder - Diagnosis and treatment - Mayo Clinic". Mayo Clinic.

"Emotion Dysregulation Treatment with DBT".

Suzer Gamli I, Tahiroglu AY (2018). "Six months methylphenidate treatment improves emotion dysregulation in adolescents with attention deficit/hyperactivity disorder: a prospective study". Neuropsychiatric Disease and Treatment. 14: 1329–1337. doi:10.2147/NDT.S164807. PMC 5973442. PMID 29872300.

Reimherr FW, Marchant BK, Strong RE, Hedges DW, Adler L, Spencer TJ, et al. (July 2005). "Emotional dysregulation in adult ADHD and response to atomoxetine". Biological Psychiatry. 58 (2): 125–31. doi:10.1016/j.biopsych.2005.04.040. PMID 16038683. S2CID 21018577.

Vacher, Cécile; Goujon, Allison; Romo, Lucia; Purper-Ouakil, Diane (2020-09-01). "Efficacy of psychosocial interventions for children with ADHD and emotion dysregulation: a systematic review". Psychiatry Research. 291: 113151. doi:10.1016/j.psychres.2020.113151. ISSN 0165-1781. PMID 32619822. S2CID 219123966.

Faraone, Stephen V.; Rostain, Anthony L.; Blader, Joseph; Busch, Betsy; Childress, Ann C.; Connor, Daniel F.; Newcorn, Jeffrey H. (February 2019). "Practitioner Review: Emotional dysregulation in attention-deficit/hyperactivity disorder - implications for clinical recognition and intervention". Journal of Child Psychology and Psychiatry. 60 (2): 133–150. doi:10.11 11/jcpp.12899. PMID 29624671.

Butler, Gillian; Hope, Tony. Managing Your Mind: The □mental fitness guide. Oxford Paperbacks, 1995

Definition of Habit. Merriam Webster Dictionary. Retrieved on August 29, 2008.

Definition of Habituation. Merriam Webster Dictionary. Retrieved on August 29, 2008

Andrews, B. R. (1903). "Habit". The American Journal of Psychology. 14 (2): 121–49. doi:10.2307/1412711. ISSN 0002-9556. JSTOR 1412711.

"Habituation." Animalbehavioronline.com. Retrieved on August 29, 2008.

Wood, W., Quinn, J. M., & Kashy, D. A. (2002). Habits in everyday life: Thought, emotion, and action. "Journal of Personality and Social Psychology". 83(6), 1281-1297. doi:10.10 37/0022-3514.83.6.1281.

Rosenthal, Norman. "Habit Formation". Sussex Directories. Retrieved November 30, 2011.

"Habit Formation". psychologytoday.com.

Wood, W.; Neal, D. T. (2007). "A new look at habits and the habit-goal interface". Psychological Review. 114 (4): 843–863. CiteSeerX 10.1.1.337.1013. doi:10.1037/0033-295X.114.4.8 43. PMID 17907866.

Bargh, J. A. (1994). "The 4 horsemen of automaticity: Awareness, intention, efficiency, and control in social cognition." In Wyer, R. S., & Srull, T. K. (Eds.), Handbook of social cognition:

Vol. 1 Basic processes, pp. 1–40. Hove: Lawrence Erlbaum Associates Publishers

"Definition of HABIT". www.merriam-webster.com. Retrieved 2021-07-07.

"The Project Gutenberg eBook of The Principles of Psychology, by William James". www.gutenberg.org. Retrieved 2021-07-07.

Hull, C. L. (1943). Principles of behavior: An introduction to behavior theory. New York: Appleton-Century-Crofts

Hull, C. L. (1951). Essentials of behavior. Westport, CT: Greenwood Press

Lally, P., van Jaarsveld, C. H. M., Potts, H. W. W., & Wardle, J. (2010). How are habits formed: Modelling habit formation in the real world. European Journal of Social Psychology. October 2010. 40(6), 998–1009. doi:10.1002/ejsp.674

Wood, W., & Neal, D. T. (2016). Healthy through habit: Interventions for initiating & maintaining health behavior change. Behavioral Science & Policy, 2(1), pp. 71–83. doi:10.1353/bsp.2016.0008

Duhigg, Charles. "Habits: How They Form And How To Break Them". NPR Fresh Air PodCast. npr. Retrieved 16 January 2021.

Wood, Wendy; Rünger, Dennis (2016). "Psychology of Habit". Annual Review of Psychology. 67: 289–314. doi:10.1146/an nurev-psych-122414-033417. PMID 26361052.

Deterding, Sebastian, et al. "Gamification. using game-design elements in non-gaming contexts." CHI'11 Extended Abstracts on Human Factors in Computing Systems. ACM, 2011.

Stawarz, K.; Cox, A. L.; Blandford, A. (2014). "Don't forget your pill!: designing effective medication reminder apps that support users' daily routines". CHI '14: Proceedings of the SIGCHI Conference on Human Factors in Computing Systems (in English and English): 2269–2278. doi:10.1145/2556 288.2557079. Wikidata Q61929041.

Stawarz, K.; Cox, A. L.; Blandford, A. (2015). Beyond Self-Tracking and Reminders: Designing Smartphone Apps That Support Habit Formation. Proceedings of the 33rd Annual ACM Conference on Human Factors in Computing Systems - CHI '15. Proceedings of the CHI Conference on Human Factors in Computing Systems (in English and English). doi:1 0.1145/2702123.2702230. ISBN 978-1-4503-3145-6. Wikidata Q61929019.

"Habits, Life, and Business - Think". www.kera.org.

Adriaanse, Marieke A.; Kroese, Floor M.; Gillebaart, Marleen; Ridder, De; D, Denise T. (2014). "Effortless inhibition: habit mediates the relation between self-control and unhealthy snack consumption". Frontiers in Psychology. 5: 444. doi:10.3389 /fpsyg.2014.00444. ISSN 1664-1078. PMC 4032877. PMID 24904463.

Schacter, Gilbert, Wegner. "Psychology Second Edition" (2011). New York: Worth Publishers.

Neal, D., Wood, W., Labrecque, J., & Lally, P. (2011). How do habits guide behavior? perceived and actual triggers of habits in daily life. Journal of Experimental Social Psychology, (48), 492-498.   Retrieved   from http://dornsife.usc.edu/assets/sites/545/docs/Wendy_Wood_ Research_Articles/Habits/neal.wood.labrecque.lally.2012_00 1_How_do_habits_guide_behavior.pdf

Anthony Dickinson (1985). Actions and Habits: The Development of Behavioural Autonomy. Philosophical Transactions of the Royal Society B: Biological Sciences, volume 308, pages 67—78. http://rstb.royalsocietypublishing.org/content/308/ 1135/67

Smith, Kyle S.; Graybiel, Ann M. (2013-07-24). "A Dual Operator View of Habitual Behavior Reflecting Cortical and Striatal Dynamics". Neuron. 79 (2): 361–374. doi:10.1016/j.n euron.2013.05.038. ISSN 0896-6273. PMC 3951965. PMID 23810540.

Payne, Arthur Frank (April 1, 1939). "The Psychology of Nervous Habits". American Journal of Orthodontics and Oral Surgery. 25 (4): 324–29. doi:10.1016/S0096-6347(39)90328-5.

"Anxiety Disorders - CMHA National". CMHA National. Retrieved 2018-02-08.

Suzanne LeVert, Gary R. McClain (2001). The Complete Idiot's Guide to Breaking Bad Habits. Alpha Books. ISBN 978-0-02-863986-4.

Murdock, KatharineThe American Journal of Nursing, V. 19 (7), 04/1919, p. 503-506

"How to Break a Bad Habit (and Replace It With a Good One)". James Clear. 2013-05-13. Retrieved 2018-02-08.

Valverde, Mariana (1998). "Disease or Habit? Alcoholism and the Exercise of Freedom". Diseases of the Will: Alcohol and the Dilemmas of Freedom. ISBN 978-0-521-64469-3.

Bas Verplanken, Suzanne Faes (21 Jun 1999). "Good intentions, bad habits, and effects of forming implementation intentions on healthy eating". European Journal of Social Psychology. 29 (5–6): 591–604. doi:10.1002/(SICI)1099-0992(199908/09)29:5/6<591::AID-EJSP948>3.0.CO;2-H. Archived from the original on 5 January 2013.

Herbert Fensterheim, Jean Baer (1975). Don't Say Yes When You Want to Say No. Dell. ISBN 978-0-440-15413-6.

"MIT explains why bad habits are hard to break". CNET. CBS Interactive.

Murdock, Katharine, The Psychology of Habit https://www.jstor.org/stable/pdf/3405395.pdf

"How Habits Work". charlesduhigg.com.

Baer, Ruth A. (2003). "Mindfulness Training as a Clinical Intervention: A Conceptual and Empirical Review" (PDF). Clinical Psychology: Science and Practice. 10 (2): 125–143. doi:10.1093/clipsy.bpg015.

Kabat-Zinn J (2013). Full Catastrophe Living: Using the Wisdom of Your Body and Mind to Face Stress, Pain, and Illness. New York: Bantam Dell. ISBN 978-0345539724.

Creswell JD (January 2017). "Mindfulness Interventions". Annual Review of Psychology. 68: 491–516. doi:10.1146/annurev-psych-042716-051139. PMID 27687118. Methodologically rigorous RCTs have demonstrated that mindfulness interventions improve outcomes in multiple domains (e.g., chronic pain, depression relapse, addiction).

Slagter HA, Davidson RJ, Lutz A (2011). "Mental training as a tool in the neuroscientific study of brain and cognitive plastici-

Polak 2011, pp. 153–56.

Williams & Tribe 2000, p. 46.

Buddhadasa Bhikkhu 2014, pp. 79, 101, 117 note 42.

Thompson, Evan (2020). Why I Am Not a Buddhist. New Haven and London: Yale University Press. p. 120. ISBN 978-0-300-22655-3. Buddhism has no single, agreed-upon traditional definition of mindfulness. Rather, Buddhism offers multiple and sometimes incompatible conceptions of mindfulness.

Anālayo B (2003). Satipaṭṭhāna, the direct path to realization. Windhorse Publications.

Buchholz L (October 2015). "Exploring the Promise of Mindfulness as Medicine". JAMA. 314 (13): 1327–1329. doi:10.10 01/jama.2015.7023. PMID 26441167.

Harrington A, Dunne JD (October 2015). "When mindfulness is therapy: Ethical qualms, historical perspectives". The American Psychologist. 70 (7): 621–631. doi:10.1037/a003 9460. PMID 26436312. S2CID 43129186. Mindfulness, the argument goes, was never supposed to be about weight loss, better sex, helping children perform better in school, helping employees be more productive in the workplace, or even improving the functioning of anxious, depressed people. It was never supposed to be a merchandized commodity to be bought and sold.

Blanck P, Perleth S, Heidenreich T, Kröger P, Ditzen B, Bents H, Mander J (March 2018). "Effects of mindfulness exercises as stand-alone intervention on symptoms of anxiety and depression: Systematic review and meta-analysis". Behaviour Research and Therapy. 102: 25–35. doi:10.1007/s12671-014-0379-y. PMID 29291584.

Khoury B, Sharma M, Rush SE, Fournier C (June 2015). "Mindfulness-based stress reduction for healthy individuals: A meta-analysis". Journal of Psychosomatic Research. 78 (6): 519–528. doi:10.1016/j.jpsychores.2015.03.009. PMID 25818837. We conducted a meta-analysis to provide a review of MBSR for healthy individuals. The meta-analysis included 29 studies enrolling 2668 participants... The results obtained are robust and are maintained at follow-up. When combined, mindfulness and compassion strongly correlated with clinical effects.

Jain FA, Walsh RN, Eisendrath SJ, Christensen S, Rael Cahn B (2015). "Critical analysis of the efficacy of meditation therapies for acute and subacute phase treatment of depressive disorders: a systematic review". Psychosomatics. 56 (2): 140–152. doi:10.1016/j.psym.2014.10.007. PMC 4383597. PMID 25591492.

Reangsing C, Punsuwun S, Schneider JK (March 2021). "Effects of mindfulness interventions on depressive symptoms in adolescents: A meta-analysis". International Journal of Nursing Studies. 115: 103848. doi:10.1016/j.ijnurstu.2020.103848. PMID 33383273. S2CID 229940390.

Sharma M, Rush SE (October 2014). "Mindfulness-based stress reduction as a stress management intervention for healthy individuals: a systematic review". Journal of Evidence-Based Complementary & Alternative Medicine. 19 (4): 271–286. doi:10.1177/2156587214543143. PMID 25053754. Mindfulness-based stress reduction offers an effective way of reducing stress by combining mindfulness meditation and yoga in an 8-week training program... Of the 17 studies, 16 demonstrated positive changes in psychological or physiological outcomes related to anxiety and/or stress. Despite the limitations of not all studies using randomized controlled design, having smaller sample sizes, and having different outcomes, mindfulness-based stress reduction appears to be a promising modality for stress management.

Hofmann et al. 2010.

Hofmann et al. 2010.

Chiesa A, Serretti A (April 2014). "Are mindfulness-based interventions effective for substance use disorders? A systematic review of the evidence". Substance Use & Misuse.

49 (5): 492–512. doi:10.3109/10826084.2013.770027. PMID 23461667. S2CID 34990668.

Garland EL, Froeliger B, Howard MO (January 2014). "Mindfulness training targets neurocognitive mechanisms of addiction at the attention-appraisal-emotion interface". Frontiers in Psychiatry. 4: 173. doi:10.3389/fpsyt.2013.00173. PMC 3887509. PMID 24454293.

Sancho M, De Gracia M, Rodríguez RC, Mallorquí-Bagué N, Sánchez-González J, Trujols J, et al. (2018). "Mindfulness-Based Interventions for the Treatment of Substance and Behavioral Addictions: A Systematic Review". Frontiers in Psychiatry. 9 (95): 95. doi:10.3389/fpsyt.2018.00095. PMC 5884944. PMID 29651257.

Noetel M, Ciarrochi J, Van Zanden B, Lonsdale C (2019). "Mindfulness and acceptance approaches to sporting performance enhancement: a systematic review". International Review of Sport and Exercise Psychology. 12 (1): 139–175. doi:10.1080/1750984X.2017.1387803. S2CID 149040404.

Paulus MP (January 2016). "Neural Basis of Mindfulness Interventions that Moderate the Impact of Stress on the Brain". Neuropsychopharmacology. 41 (1): 373. doi:10.1038/npp.2015.239. PMC 4677133. PMID 26657952.

Dunning DL, Griffiths K, Kuyken W, Crane C, Foulkes L, Parker J, Dalgleish T (March 2019). "Research Review: The effects of mindfulness-based interventions on cognition and mental health in children and adolescents - a meta-analysis of randomized controlled trials". Journal of Child Psychology and Psychiatry, and Allied Disciplines. 60 (3): 244–258. doi:10.11 11/jcpp.12980. PMC 6546608. PMID 30345511.

Tomlinson ER, Yousaf O, Vittersø AD, Jones L (2018). "Dispositional Mindfulness and Psychological Health: a Systematic Review". Mindfulness. 9 (1): 23–43. doi:10.1007/s12671-017 -0762-6. PMC 5770488. PMID 29387263.

Keng SL, Smoski MJ, Robins CJ (August 2011). "Effects of mindfulness on psychological health: a review of empirical studies". Clinical Psychology Review. 31 (6): 1041–1056. doi: 10.1016/j.cpr.2011.04.006. PMC 3679190. PMID 21802619.

Goldberg SB, Tucker RP, Greene PA, Davidson RJ, Wampold BE, Kearney DJ, Simpson TL (February 2018). "Mindfulness-based interventions for psychiatric disorders: A systematic review and meta-analysis". Clinical Psychology Review. 59: 52–60. doi:10.1016/j.cpr.2017.10.011. PMC 5741505. PMID 29126747.

Boyd JE, Lanius RA, McKinnon MC (January 2018). "Mindfulness-based treatments for posttraumatic stress disorder: a review of the treatment literature and neurobiological evidence".

Journal of Psychiatry & Neuroscience. 43 (1): 7–25. doi:10.1503/jpn.170021. PMC 5747539. PMID 29252162.

Rodrigues MF, Nardi AE, Levitan M (2017). "Mindfulness in mood and anxiety disorders: a review of the literature". Trends in Psychiatry and Psychotherapy. 39 (3): 207–215. doi:10.1590/2237-6089-2016-0051. PMID 28767927.

Aust J, Bradshaw T (February 2017). "Mindfulness interventions for psychosis: a systematic review of the literature". Journal of Psychiatric and Mental Health Nursing. 24 (1): 69–83. doi:10.1111/jpm.12357. PMID 27928859. S2CID 206143093.

Cramer H, Lauche R, Haller H, Langhorst J, Dobos G (January 2016). "Mindfulness- and Acceptance-based Interventions for Psychosis: A Systematic Review and Meta-analysis". Global Advances in Health and Medicine. 5 (1): 30–43. doi:10.7453/gahmj.2015.083. PMC 4756771. PMID 26937312. Moderate evidence was found for short-term effects on total psychotic symptoms, positive symptoms, hospitalization rates, duration of hospitalization, and mindfulness and for long-term effects on total psychotic symptoms and duration of hospitalization.

Louise S, Fitzpatrick M, Strauss C, Rossell SL, Thomas N (February 2018). "Mindfulness- and acceptance-based interventions for psychosis: Our current understanding and a meta-analysis". Schizophrenia Research. 192: 57–63. doi:10.1016/j.schres.2017.05.023. PMID 28545945. S2CID 3374099.

Kaplan DM, Palitsky R, Carey AL, Crane TE, Havens CM, Medrano MR, et al. (July 2018). "Maladaptive repetitive thought as a transdiagnostic phenomenon and treatment target: An integrative review". Journal of Clinical Psychology. 74 (7): 1126–1136. doi:10.1002/jclp.22585. PMID 29342312.

Watkins E (2015). "Psychological treatment of depressive rumination". Current Opinion in Psychology. 4: 32–36. doi:10.1016/j.copsyc.2015.01.020. hdl:10871/17315.

Querstret D, Cropley M (December 2013). "Assessing treatments used to reduce rumination and/or worry: a systematic review". Clinical Psychology Review. 33 (8): 996–1009. doi:10.1016/j.cpr.2013.08.004. hdl:2164/3892. PMID 24036088.

Kiken LG, Garland EL, Bluth K, Palsson OS, Gaylord SA (July 2015). "From a state to a trait: Trajectories of state mindfulness in meditation during intervention predict changes in trait mindfulness". Personality and Individual Differences. Dr. Sybil Eysenck Young Researcher Award. 81: 41–46. doi:10.1016/j.paid.2014.12.044. PMC 4404745. PMID 25914434.

Gu J, Strauss C, Bond R, Cavanagh K (April 2015). "How do mindfulness-based cognitive therapy and mindfulness-based stress reduction improve mental health and wellbeing? A systematic review and meta-analysis of mediation studies". Clinical Psychology Review. 37: 1–12. doi:10.1016/j.cpr.2015.01.006. PMID 25689576.

Perestelo-Perez L, Barraca J, Peñate W, Rivero-Santana A, Alvarez-Perez Y (2017). "Mindfulness-based interventions for the treatment of depressive rumination: Systematic review and meta-analysis". International Journal of Clinical and Health Psychology. 17 (3): 282–295. doi:10.1016/j.ijchp.2017.07.00 4. PMC 6220915. PMID 30487903.

Tang YY, Leve LD (March 2016). "A translational neuroscience perspective on mindfulness meditation as a prevention strategy". Translational Behavioral Medicine. 6 (1): 63–72. doi:10.1 007/s13142-015-0360-x. PMC 4807201. PMID 27012254.

Cheng FK (2016). "Is meditation conducive to mental well-being for adolescents? An integrative review for mental health nursing". International Journal of Africa Nursing Sciences. 4: 7–19. doi:10.1016/j.ijans.2016.01.001.

Britton WB (August 2019). "Can mindfulness be too much of a good thing? The value of a middle way". Current Opinion in Psychology. 28: 159–165. doi:10.1016/j.copsyc.2018.12.01 1. PMC 6612475. PMID 30708288.

David Creswell, J.; Lindsay, Emily K.; Villalba, Daniella K.; Chin, Brian (April 1, 2020). "Mindfulness Training and Physical Health: Mechanisms and Outcomes". Psychosomatic Medicine. 81 (3): 224–232. doi:10.1097/PSY.0000000000000675. ISSN 0033-3174. PMC 6613793. PMID 30806634.

Karunamuni N, Imayama I, Goonetilleke D (March 2021). "Pathways to well-being: Untangling the causal relationships among biopsychosocial variables". Social Science & Medicine. 272: 112846. doi:10.1016/j.socscimed.2020.112846. PMID 32089388. S2CID 211262159.

Grierson AB, Hickie IB, Naismith SL, Scott J (September 2016). "The role of rumination in illness trajectories in youth: linking trans-diagnostic processes with clinical staging models". Psychological Medicine. 46 (12): 2467–2484. doi:10.1017/S0033291716001392. PMC 4988274. PMID 27352637.

Verkuil B, Brosschot JF, Gebhardt WA, Thayer JF (2010). "When worries make you sick: a review of perseverative cognition, the default stress response and somatic health". J. Exp. Psychopathol. 1 (1): 87–118. doi:10.5127/jep.009110.

Pascoe MC, Thompson DR, Jenkins ZM, Ski CF (December 2017). "Mindfulness mediates the physiological markers of stress: Systematic review and meta-analysis". Journal of Psychiatric Research. 95: 156–178. doi:10.1016/j.jpsychires.2017.08.004. PMID 28863392.

Dunn, Thomas J.; Dimolareva, Mirena (March 2022). "The effect of mindfulness-based interventions on immunity-related biomarkers: a comprehensive meta-analysis of randomised controlled trials". Clinical Psychology Review. 92:

ness-Based Interventions for Adults with Cardiovascular Disease: A Systematic Review and Meta-Analysis". Annals of Behavioral Medicine. 54 (1): 67–73. doi:10.1093/abm/kaz020. PMC 6922300. PMID 31167026.

Schutte NS, Malouff JM (April 2014). "A meta-analytic review of the effects of mindfulness meditation on telomerase activity". Psychoneuroendocrinology. 42: 45–48. doi:10.1016/j.psyneu en.2013.12.017. PMID 24636500. S2CID 39094183.

Borquist-Conlon, Debra S.; Maynard, Brandy R.; Brendel, Kristen Esposito; Farina, Anne S. J. (February 2019). "Mindfulness-Based Interventions for Youth With Anxiety: A Systematic Review and Meta-Analysis". Research on Social Work Practice. 29 (2): 195–205. doi:10.1177/1049731516684961 . S2CID 151941817.

Zoogman, Sarah; Goldberg, Simon B.; Hoyt, William T.; Miller, Lisa (April 2015). "Mindfulness Interventions with Youth: A Meta-Analysis". Mindfulness. 6 (2): 290–302. doi:10.1007/s1 2671-013-0260-4. S2CID 30942684.

McKeering, Phillipa; Hwang, Yoon-Suk (April 2019). "A Systematic Review of Mindfulness-Based School Interventions with Early Adolescents". Mindfulness. 10 (4): 593–610. doi: 10.1007/s12671-018-0998-9. S2CID 149885706.

Montero-Marin, Jesus; Allwood, Matthew; Ball, Susan; Crane, Catherine; Wilde, Katherine De; Hinze, Verena; Jones, Benjamin; Lord, Liz; Nuthall, Elizabeth; Raja, Anam; Taylor, Laura (July 7, 2022). "School-based mindfulness training in early adolescence: what works, for whom and how in the MYRIAD trial?". Evidence-Based Mental Health. 25 (3): 117–124. doi:10.1136/ebmental-2022-300439. ISSN 1362-0347. PMC 9340034. PMID 35820993.

Gunaratana B (2011). Mindfulness in plain English (PDF). Boston: Wisdom Publications. p. 21. ISBN 978-0861719068. Archived from the original (PDF) on 2017-12-15. Retrieved 2015-01-30.

Kabat-Zinn himself, in Full Catastrophe Living (Revised Edition) (2013), p. lxiv

"7 Tips to Balance Your Work & Life with Mindfulness". mindfulleader.org. Retrieved 2021-06-03.

Wilson 2014, p. [page needed].

Ihnen & Flynn 2008, p. 148.

Teasdale & Segal 2007, pp. 55–56.

Stanszus LS, Frank P, Geiger SM (October 2019). "Healthy eating and sustainable nutrition through mindfulness? Mixed method results of a controlled intervention study". Appetite. 141: 104325. doi:10.1016/j.appet.2019.104325. PMID 31228507. S2CID 195063688.

Pickert K (February 2014). "The art of being mindful. Finding peace in a stressed-out, digitally dependent culture may just be a matter of thinking differently". Time. Vol. 183, no. 4. pp. 40–46. PMID 24640415.

Wilson 2014, pp. 54–55.

Mahāsi Sayādaw, Manual of Insight, Chapter 5

Mahasi Sayadaw, Practical Vipassana Instructions, pp. 22–27

"The Art of Living: Vipassana Meditation". Dhamma.org. Retrieved 2013-05-30.

Karunamuni ND (2015). "The Five-Aggregate Model of the Mind". SAGE Open. 5 (2): 215824401558386. doi:10.1177/2158244015583860.

Brown KW, Ryan RM, Creswell JD (2007). "Mindfulness: Theoretical Foundations and Evidence for its Salutary Effects". Psychological Inquiry. 18 (4): 211–37. doi:10.1080/10478400701598298. S2CID 2755919.

Sharf 2014, p. 942.

Levman, Bryan (2017). "Putting smṛti back into sati (Putting remembrance back into mindfulness)". Journal of the Oxford Centre for Buddhist Studies. 13: 121 at 122.

Sharf 2014, pp. 942–943.

Sharf 2014, p. 943.

"Is Mindfulness Present-Centered and Nonjudgmental? A Discussion of the Cognitive Dimensions of Mindfulness" by Georges Dreyfus

"Mindfulness and Ethics: Attention, Virtue and Perfection" by Jay Garfield

Davids TR (1881). Buddhist Suttas. Clarendon Press. p. 107. OCLC 13247398.

Gogerly, D.J. (1845). "On Buddhism". Journal of the Ceylon Branch of the Royal Asiatic Society. 1: 7–28.

Davids TR (1881). Buddhist Suttas. Clarendon Press. p. 145. OCLC 13247398.

"Lecture, Stanford University Center for Compassion and Altruism Research and Education". The Center for Compassion and Altruism Research and Education. 2011. Archived from the original on 2012-11-20.

James H. Austin (2014), Zen-Brain Horizons: Toward a Living Zen, MIT Press, p. 83

Hayes AM (2004). "Clarifying the Construct of Mindfulness in the Context of Emotion Regulation and the Process of Change in Therapy". Clinical Psychology: Science and Practice. 11 (3): 255–62. CiteSeerX 10.1.1.168.5070. doi:10.1093/clipsy/bph 080.

Gehart 2012, pp. 7–8.

Black 2011, p. 1.

Black 2011, p. 2.

Gehart 2012, p. 7.

Zgierska et al. 2009.

Didonna 2008, p. 27.

Kristeller 2007, p. 393.

Germer 2005, p. 15.

Hick 2010, p. 10.

Bishop et al. 2004.

Tanay & Bernstein 2013, pp. 1286–1299.[page range too broad]

Marlatt & Kristeller 1999, p. 68.

Hick 2010, p. 6.

Yates, John; Immergut, Matthew; Graves, Jeremy (2015). The Mind Illuminated. Hay House. p. 30.

Bhante, Vimalaramsi (2015). A Guide to Tranquil Wisdom Insight Meditation (PDF). Annapolis, MO: CreateSpace Independent Publishing Platform. p. 4. ISBN 978-1508569718.

Oxford English Dictionary, second ed., 2002

Kabat-Zinn 2011, pp. 22–23.

Kabat-Zinn, Jon (2013). Arriving at Your Own Door: 108 Lessons in Mindfulness. Hyperion. p. 65. ISBN 978-1306752299.

Bishop et al. 2004, p. 232.

Bishop et al. 2004, p. 233.

McMahan 2008.

Sharf 1995.

"The 18th Mind and Life Dialogues meeting". Archived from the original on 2014-03-22. Retrieved 2018-01-07.

Vetter 1988.

Rhys Davids T (1959) [1910]. Dialogues of the Buddha, Part II. Oxford, Great Britain: Pali Text Society. pp. 322–346. ISBN 0-86013-034-7.

Warner B (2003). Hardcore Zen: Punk Rock, Monster Movies, & the Truth about Reality. Wisdom Publications. pp. 189–190. ISBN 086171380X.

Suzuki S (2011). Zen Mind, Beginner's Mind. Shambhala Publications. pp. 15–16. ISBN 978-159030849-3.

"What is Theravada Buddhism?". Access to Insight. Retrieved 2013-08-17.

""The Nature of Mindfulness and Its Role in Buddhist Meditation" A Correspondence between B.A. wallace and the Venerable Bikkhu Bodhi, Winter 2006, p.4" (PDF). Retrieved 2018-01-07.

Buddhadasa Bhikkhu (2014), Heartwood of the Bodhi Tree, Wisdom publications, pp. 79, 101, 117 note 42

Polak 2011.

Repetti 2022.

Lee 2020, p. 363.

"The Spiritual Exercises of St. Ignatius of Loyola: Third Week: Eating".

Harris 2009, p. 268.

Kipf 1979, pp. 3–8.

King 2001.

Wilson 2014, p. 22.

Wilson 2014, p. 17.

Bishop et al. 2004, pp. 230–231: "Much of the interest in the clinical applications of mindfulness has been sparked by the introduction of Mindfulness-Based Stress Reduction (MBSR), a manualized treatment program originally developed for the management of chronic pain (Kabat-Zinn, 1982; Kabat-Zinn, Lipworth, & Burney, 1985; Kabat-Zinn, Lipworth, Burney, & Sellers, 1987)."

James, William (2012). Bradley, Matthew (ed.). The Varieties of Religious Experience. Oxford University Press.

Valerio A (2016). "Owning Mindfulness: A Bibliometric Analysis of Mindfulness Literature Trends Within and Outside of Buddhist Contexts". Contemporary Buddhism. 17: 157–83. doi:10.1080/14639947.2016.1162425. S2CID 148411457.

Kabat-Zinn 2000.

Ergas O (2013). "Mindfulness in education at the intersection of science, religion, and healing". Critical Studies in Education. 55: 58–72. doi:10.1080/17508487.2014.858643. S2CID 144860756.

Piet J, Hougaard E (August 2011). "The effect of mindfulness-based cognitive therapy for prevention of relapse in recurrent major depressive disorder: a systematic review and meta-analysis". Clinical Psychology Review. 31 (6): 1032–1040. doi:10.1016/j.cpr.2011.05.002. PMID 21802618.

Manicavasgar V, Parker G, Perich T (April 2011). "Mindfulness-based cognitive therapy vs cognitive behaviour therapy as a treatment for non-melancholic depression". Journal of Affective Disorders. 130 (1–2): 138–144. doi:10.1016/j.jad.2010.09.027. PMID 21093925.

Hofmann SG, Sawyer AT, Fang A (September 2010). "The empirical status of the "new wave" of cognitive behavioral therapy". The Psychiatric Clinics of North America. 33 (3): 701–710. doi:10.1016/j.psc.2010.04.006. PMC 2898899. PMID 20599141.

Felder JN, Dimidjian S, Segal Z (February 2012). "Collaboration in mindfulness-based cognitive therapy". Journal of Clinical Psychology. 68 (2): 179–186. doi:10.1002/jclp.21832. PMID 23616298.

Ma SH, Teasdale JD (February 2004). "Mindfulness-based cognitive therapy for depression: replication and exploration of

Llácer, Lorena Alonso; Ramos-Campos, Marta (2018). "Mindfulness y Cáncer: Aplicación del programa MBPM de Respira Vida Breatworks en pacientes oncol'ógicos". Revista de Investigación y Educación en Ciencias de la Salud (in Spanish). 3 (2): 33–45. doi:10.37536/RIECS.2018.3.2.101. ISSN 2530-2787.

Agostinis, Alessio; Barrow, Michelle; Taylor, Chad; Gray, Callum (2017). Self-Selection all the Way: Improving Patients' Pain Experience and Outcomes on a Pilot Breathworks Mindfulness for Health Programme.

Long J, Briggs M, Long A, Astin F (October 2016). "Starting where I am: a grounded theory exploration of mindfulness as a facilitator of transition in living with a long-term condition" (PDF). Journal of Advanced Nursing. 72 (10): 2445–2456. doi:10.1111/jan.12998. PMID 27174075. S2CID 4917280.

Doran NJ (June 2014). "Experiencing Wellness Within Illness: Exploring a Mindfulness-Based Approach to Chronic Back Pain". Qualitative Health Research. 24 (6): 749–760. doi:10.1177/1049732314529662. PMID 24728110. S2CID 45682942.

Brown CA, Jones AK (March 2013). "Psychobiological correlates of improved mental health in patients with musculoskeletal pain after a mindfulness-based pain management program". The Clinical Journal of Pain. 29 (3): 233–244. doi:10.1097/AJP.0b013e31824c5d9f. PMID 22874090. S2CID 33688569.

Plumb JC, Stewart I, Dahl J, Lundgren T (2009). "In search of meaning: values in modern clinical behavior analysis". The Behavior Analyst. 32 (1): 85–103. doi:10.1007/bf03392177. PMC 2686995. PMID 22478515.

Hayes S. "Acceptance & Commitment Therapy (ACT)". Con textualPsychology.org.

Zettle RD (2005). "The evolution of a contextual approach to therapy: From comprehensive distancing to ACT". International Journal of Behavioral Consultation and Therapy. 1 (2): 77–89. doi:10.1037/h0100736. S2CID 4835864.

Murdock, N. L. (2009). Theories of counseling and psychotherapy: A case approach. Upper Saddle River, N.J: Merrill/Pearson

"Getting in on the Act - The Irish Times - Tue, Jun 07, 2011". The Irish Times. June 7, 2011. Retrieved 2012-03-16.

Linehan 1993, p. 19.

Linehan 1993, pp. 20–21.

Apsche JA, DiMeo L (2010). Mode Deactivation Therapy for aggression and oppositional behavior in adolescents: An integrative methodology using ACT, DBT, and CBT. Oakland, CA: New Harbinger. ISBN 978-1608821075.

Swart J, Apsche J (2014). "Family mode deactivation therapy (FMDT) mediation analysis". International Journal of Behavioral Consultation and Therapy. 9: 1–13. doi:10.1037/h0101 009.

McCracken, Gauntlett-Gilbert & Vowles 2007.

Grossman et al. 2004.

Melemis 2008, pp. 141–157.

Williams et al. 2006.

Bell 2009.

Sugg HV, Frost J, Richards DA (May 2019). "Morita Therapy for depression (Morita Trial): an embedded qualitative study of acceptability". BMJ Open. 9 (5): e023873. doi:10.1136/bmjo pen-2018-023873. PMC 6549637. PMID 31147359.

"Mindfulness and CBT". Archived from the original on 2020-02-02. Retrieved 2020-02-02.

Kurtz R (1990). Body-Centered Psychotherapy, The Hakomi Method. LifeRhythm.

Schwartz RC (2013). Internal Family Systems Therapy. Guilford Publications. ISBN 978-1462513956.

Robinson L, Segal R, Segal J, Smith M (December 2017). "Relaxation Techniques". Helpguide.org.

"Mindful Kids Miami, Inc | Mindful Miami". Mindful Kids Miami.

"Susan Kaiser Greenland -- Inner Kids". Archived from the original on 2010-04-23.

"MindUP™". Archived from the original on 2015-04-17. Retrieved 2015-04-17.

"Mindful Moment Program". Retrieved 2020-02-02.

Ergas O, Todd S, eds. (2016). Philosophy East/West: Exploring intersections between educational and contemplative practices (1st ed.). Wiley-Blackwell. ISBN 978-1-119-14733-6.[page needed]

j. Davidson, Richard; Dunne, John; Eccles, Jacquelynne S.; Engle, Adam; Greenberg, Mark; Jennings, Patricia; Jha, Amishi; Jinpa, Thupten; Lantieri, Linda; Meyer, David; Roeser, Robert W.; Vago, David (June 2012). "Contemplative Practices and Mental Training: Prospects for American Education". Child Development Perspectives. 6 (2): 146–153. doi:10.1111/j.1750-8606.2012.00240.x. PMC 3420012. PMID 22905038.

Hobby K, Jenkins E (2014). "Mindfulness in schools". Earth-Song Journal. 2 (7): 26. ISSN 1449-8367.

Zenner C, Herrnleben-Kurz S, Walach H (2014). "Mindfulness-based interventions in schools-a systematic review and meta-analysis". Frontiers in Psychology. 5: 603. doi:10.3389/fpsyg.2014.00603. PMC 4075476. PMID 25071620.

Renshaw TL, Cook CR (2017). "Introduction to the Special Issue: Mindfulness in the Schools-Historical Roots, Current Status, and Future Directions". Psychology in the Schools. 54: 5–12. doi:10.1002/pits.21978.

Eklund K, O'Malley M, Meyer L (2017). "Gauging Mindfulness in Children and Youth: School-Based Applications". Psychology in the Schools. 54: 101–14. doi:10.1002/pits.21983.

McKeering, Phillipa; Hwang, Yoon-Suk (July 18, 2018). "A Systematic Review of Mindfulness-Based School Interventions with Early Adolescents". Mindfulness. 10 (4): 593–610. doi:10.1007/s12671-018-0998-9.

Choudhury S, Moses JM (2016). "Mindful interventions: Youth, poverty, and the developing brain". Theory & Psychology. 26 (5): 591–606. doi:10.1177/0959354316669025. S2CID 151984948.

Semple RJ, Lee J, Rosa D, Miller LF (2009). "A Randomized Trial of Mindfulness-Based Cognitive Therapy for Children: Promoting Mindful Attention to Enhance Social-Emotional Resiliency in Children". Journal of Child and Family Studies. 19 (2): 218–29. doi:10.1007/s10826-009-9301-y. S2CID 143769629.

Flook L, Smalley SL, Kitil MJ, Galla BM, Kaiser-Greenland S, Locke J, Ishijima E, Kasari C (2010). "Effects of Mindful Awareness Practices on Executive Functions in Elementary School Children". Journal of Applied School Psychology. 26 (1): 70–95. doi:10.1080/15377900903379125. S2CID 16258631.

Kuyken W, Weare K, Ukoumunne OC, Vicary R, Motton N, Burnett R, et al. (August 2013). "Effectiveness of the Mindfulness in Schools Programme: non-randomised controlled feasibility study". The British Journal of Psychiatry. 203 (2): 126–131. doi:10.1192/bjp.bp.113.126649. hdl:10871/11441. PMID 23787061. S2CID 13942589.

Johnson C, Burke C, Brinkman S, Wade T (June 2016). "Effectiveness of a school-based mindfulness program for transdiagnostic prevention in young adolescents". Behaviour Research and Therapy. 81: 1–11. doi:10.1016/j.brat.2016.03.002. PMID 27054828.

Good DJ, Lyddy CJ, Glomb TM, Bono JE, Brown KW, Duffy MK, Baer RA, Brewer JA, Lazar SW (2015). "Contemplating Mindfulness at Work". Journal of Management. 42 (1): 114–42. doi:10.1177/0149206315617003. S2CID 15676226.

Boyatzis, R. E., & McKee, A. (2005). Resonant Leadership: Renewing yourself and connecting with others through mindfulness, hope, and compassion. Boston: Harvard Business School Press.

Carroll M (2007). The Mindful Leader: Ten Principles for Bringing Out the Best in Ourselves and Others. Shambhala Publications. ISBN 9781590303474.

Schultz PP, Ryan RM, Niemiec CP, Legate N, Williams GC (2014). "Mindfulness, Work Climate, and Psychological Need Satisfaction in Employee Well-being". Mindfulness. 6 (5): 971. doi:10.1007/s12671-014-0338-7. S2CID 145360486.

Janssen M, Heerkens Y, Kuijer W, van der Heijden B, Engels J (2018). "Effects of Mindfulness-Based Stress Reduction on employees' mental health: A systematic review". PLOS ONE. 13 (1): e0191332. Bibcode:2018PLoSO..1391332J. doi:10.1371/journal.pone.0191332. PMC 5783379. PMID 29364935.

Meditation classes raise attorneys mindfulness (2009). New Orleans CityBusiness.

Program on Negotiation at Harvard Law School (2008). Program on Negotiation Webcasts.

Samuelson M, Carmody J, Kabat-Zinn J, Bratt MA (2016). "Mindfulness-Based Stress Reduction in Massachusetts Cor-

rectional Facilities". The Prison Journal. 87 (2): 254–68. doi
:10.1177/0032885507303753. S2CID 51730633.

Shonin E, Van Gordon W, Slade K, Griffiths MD (2013).
"Mindfulness and other Buddhist-derived interventions in correctional settings: A systematic review" (PDF). Aggression and
Violent Behavior. 18 (3): 365–72. doi:10.1016/j.avb.2013.01.
002.

Dafoe T, Stermac L (2013). "Mindfulness Meditation as an
Adjunct Approach to Treatment Within the Correctional System". Journal of Offender Rehabilitation. 52 (3): 198–216. d
oi:10.1080/10509674.2012.752774. S2CID 144734159.

Rochman B (September 6, 2009). "Samurai Mind Training for
Modern American Warriors.". Time.

Sequeira S (January 2014). "Foreword to Advances in Meditation Research: neuroscience and clinical applications". Annals
of the New York Academy of Sciences. 1307 (1): v–vi. Bibc
ode:2014NYASA1307D...5S. doi:10.1111/nyas.12305. PMID
24571183. S2CID 30918843.

Vonderlin, Ruben; Biermann, Miriam; Bohus, Martin;
Lyssenko, Lisa (March 2, 2020). "Mindfulness-Based Programs
in the Workplace: a Meta-Analysis of Randomized Controlled
Trials". Mindfulness. 11 (7): 1579–1598. doi:10.1007/s12671
-020-01328-3.

Dawson AF, Brown WW, Anderson J, Datta B, Donald JN, Hong K, et al. (July 2020). "Mindfulness-Based Interventions for University Students: A Systematic Review and Meta-Analysis of Randomised Controlled Trials". Applied Psychology: Health and Well-Being. 12 (2): 384–410. doi:10.1111/aphw.12188. PMID 31743957. S2CID 208186271.

Sala M, Shankar Ram S, Vanzhula IA, Levinson CA (June 2020). "Mindfulness and eating disorder psychopathology: A meta-analysis". The International Journal of Eating Disorders. 53 (6): 834–851. doi:10.1002/eat.23247. PMID 32100320.

Carrière K, Khoury B, Günak MM, Knäuper B (February 2018). "Mindfulness-based interventions for weight loss: a systematic review and meta-analysis". Obesity Reviews. 19 (2): 164–177. doi:10.1111/obr.12623. PMID 29076610. S2CID 44877765.

Rogers JM, Ferrari M, Mosely K, Lang CP, Brennan L (January 2017). "Mindfulness-based interventions for adults who are overweight or obese: a meta-analysis of physical and psychological health outcomes". Obesity Reviews. 18 (1): 51–67. doi:10.1111/obr.12461. hdl:10072/393029. PMID 27862826. S2CID 3977651.

Xue J, Zhang Y, Huang Y (June 2019). "A meta-analytic investigation of the impact of mindfulness-based interventions on differential relapse prevention effects". Journal of Consulting and Clinical Psychology. 72 (1): 31–40. CiteSeerX 10.1.1.47 6.9744. doi:10.1037/0022-006x.72.1.31. PMID 14756612.

Cusens B, Duggan GB, Thorne K, Burch V (2010). "Evaluation of the breathworks mindfulness-based pain management programme: effects on well-being and multiple measures of mindfulness". Clinical Psychology & Psychotherapy. 17 (1): 63–78. doi:10.1002/cpp.653. PMID 19911432.

Pizutti LT, Carissimi A, Valdivia LJ, Ilgenfritz CA, Freitas JJ, Sopezki D, et al. (June 2019). "Evaluation of Breathworks' Mindfulness for Stress 8-week course: Effects on depressive symptoms, psychiatric symptoms, affects, self-compassion, and mindfulness facets in Brazilian health professionals". Journal of Clinical Psychology. 75 (6): 970–984. doi:10.1002/jclp.22749. PMID 30689206. S2CID 59306658.

Mehan, Suraj; Morris, Julia (2018). "A literature review of Breathworks and mindfulness intervention". British Journal of Healthcare Management. 24 (5): 235–241. doi:10.12968/bjh c.2018.24.5.235. ISSN 1358-0574.

Lopes SA, Vannucchi BP, Demarzo M, Cunha ÂG, Nunes MD (February 2019). "Effectiveness of a Mindfulness-Based Intervention in the Management of Musculoskeletal Pain in Nursing Workers". Pain Management Nursing. 20 (1): 32–38. doi:10.1 016/j.pmn.2018.02.065. PMID 29779791. S2CID 29170927.

ADHD symptoms". Medicine. 98 (23): e15957. doi:10.1097 /MD.0000000000015957. PMC 6571280. PMID 31169722.

Cavicchioli M, Movalli M, Maffei C (2018). "The Clinical Efficacy of Mindfulness-Based Treatments for Alcohol and Drugs Use Disorders: A Meta-Analytic Review of Randomized and Nonrandomized Controlled Trials". European Addiction Research. 24 (3): 137–162. doi:10.1159/000490762. PMID 30016796.

Spijkerman MP, Pots WT, Bohlmeijer ET (April 2016). "Effectiveness of online mindfulness-based interventions in improving mental health: A review and meta-analysis of randomised controlled trials". Clinical Psychology Review. 45: 102–114. doi:10.1016/j.cpr.2016.03.009. PMID 27111302.

Wang YY, Wang F, Zheng W, Zhang L, Ng CH, Ungvari GS, Xiang YT (2020). "Mindfulness-Based Interventions for Insomnia: A Meta-Analysis of Randomized Controlled Trials". Behavioral Sleep Medicine. 18 (1): 1–9. doi:10.1080/154020 02.2018.1518228. PMID 30380915. S2CID 53201885.

Kanen, Jonathan; Nazir, Racha; Sedky, Karim; Pradhan, Basant (April 30, 2015). "The Effects of Mindfulness-Based Interventions on Sleep Disturbance: A Meta-Analysis". Adolescent Psychiatry. 5 (2): 105–115. doi:10.2174/2210676605666150311 222928.

"The Science of Relaxation - Lectures by neuroscientist Martin Dresler and psychiatrist Anne Speckens". Radboud Reflects and Donders Institute. December 9, 2020. Archived from the original on 2021-12-22.

Xunlin NG, Lau Y, Klainin-Yobas P (April 2020). "The effectiveness of mindfulness-based interventions among cancer patients and survivors: a systematic review and meta-analysis". Supportive Care in Cancer. 28 (4): 1563–1578. doi:10.1007/s00520-019-05219-9. PMID 31834518. S2CID 209331542.

Xie C, Dong B, Wang L, Jing X, Wu Y, Lin L, Tian L (March 2020). "Mindfulness-based stress reduction can alleviate cancer- related fatigue: A meta-analysis". Journal of Psychosomatic Research. 130: 109916. doi:10.1016/j.jpsychores.2019.109916. PMID 31927347. S2CID 210166679.

Nnate DA, Anyachukwu CC, Igwe SE, Abaraogu UO (October 2021). "Mindfulness-based interventions for psychological wellbeing and quality of life in men with prostate cancer: A systematic review and meta-analysis". Psycho-Oncology. 30 (10): 1680–1690. doi:10.1002/pon.5749. PMID 34139035. S2CID 235470939.

Cillessen L, Johannsen M, Speckens AE, Zachariae R (December 2019). "Mindfulness-based interventions for psychological and physical health outcomes in cancer patients and survivors: A systematic review and meta-analysis of randomized

controlled trials". Psycho-Oncology. 28 (12): 2257–2269. do
i:10.1002/pon.5214. PMC 6916350. PMID 31464026.

Benevides TW, Shore SM, Andresen ML, Caplan R, Cook B,
Gassner DL, et al. (August 2020). "Interventions to address
health outcomes among autistic adults: A systematic review".
Autism. 24 (6): 1345–1359. doi:10.1177/1362361320913664.
PMC 7787674. PMID 32390461.

Simpson R, Simpson S, Ramparsad N, Lawrence M, Booth
J, Mercer SW (February 2020). "Effects of Mindfulness-based
interventions on physical symptoms in people with multiple
sclerosis - a systematic review and meta-analysis" (PDF). Multiple Sclerosis and Related Disorders. 38: 101493. doi:10.1016/
j.msard.2019.101493. PMID 31835209. S2CID 209232064.

Di Cara M, Grezzo D, Palmeri R, Lo Buono V, Cartella E,
Micchia K, et al. (January 2022). "Psychological well-being in
people with multiple sclerosis: a descriptive review of the ef-
fects obtained with mindfulness interventions". Neurological
Sciences. 43 (1): 211–217. doi:10.1007/s10072-021-05686-1.
PMC 8724219. PMID 34697659.

DiRenzo D, Crespo-Bosque M, Gould N, Finan P, Nana-
vati J, Bingham CO (October 2018). "Systematic Review and
Meta-analysis: Mindfulness-Based Interventions for Rheuma-
toid Arthritis". Current Rheumatology Reports. 20 (12):

75. doi:10.1007/s11926-018-0787-4. PMC 6233984. PMID 30338418.

Guo J, Wang H, Luo J, Guo Y, Xie Y, Lei B, et al. (December 11, 2019). "Factors influencing the effect of mindfulness-based interventions on diabetes distress: a meta-analysis". BMJ Open Diabetes Research & Care. 7 (1): e000757. doi:10.1136/bmjdrc-2019-000757. PMC 6936501. PMID 31908794.

Demarzo MM, Montero-Marin J, Cuijpers P, Zabaleta-del-Olmo E, Mahtani KR, Vellinga A, et al. (November 2015). "The Efficacy of Mindfulness-Based Interventions in Primary Care: A Meta-Analytic Review". Annals of Family Medicine. 13 (6): 573–582. doi:10.1370/afm.1863. PMC 4639383. PMID 26553897.

Goyal M, Singh S, Sibinga EM, Gould NF, Rowland-Seymour A, Sharma R, et al. (March 2014). "Meditation programs for psychological stress and well-being: a systematic review and meta-analysis". JAMA Internal Medicine. 174 (3): 357–368. doi:10.1001/jamainternmed.2013.13018. PMC 4142584. PMID 24395196.

Tang YY, Hölzel BK, Posner MI (April 2015). "The neuroscience of mindfulness meditation". Nature Reviews. Neuroscience. 16 (4): 213–225. doi:10.1038/nrn3916. PMID 25783612. S2CID 54521922.

Colzato LS, Kibele A (2017). "How Different Types of Meditation Can Enhance Athletic Performance Depending on the Specific Sport Skills". Journal of Cognitive Enhancement. 1 (2): 122–26. doi:10.1007/s41465-017-0018-3.

Petcharat M, Liehr P (February 2017). "Mindfulness training for parents of children with special needs: Guidance for nurses in mental health practice". Journal of Child and Adolescent Psychiatric Nursing. 30 (1): 35–46. doi:10.1111/jcap.12169. PMID 28449389. S2CID 3775407.

Fuchs WW, Mundschenk NJ, Groark B (2017). "A Promising Practice: School-Based Mindfulness-Based Stress Reduction for Children with Disabilities". Journal of International Special Needs Education. 20 (2): 56–66. doi:10.9782/2159-4341-20.2.56. S2CID 152021458.

Cachia RL, Anderson A, Moore DW (2016). "Mindfulness in Individuals with Autism Spectrum Disorder: A Systematic Review and Narrative Analysis". Review Journal of Autism and Developmental Disorders. 3 (2): 165–78. doi:10.1007/s40489-016-0074-0. S2CID 146901638.

Garland SN, Zhou ES, Gonzalez BD, Rodriguez N (September 2016). "The Quest for Mindful Sleep: A Critical Synthesis of the Impact of Mindfulness-Based Interventions for Insomnia". Current Sleep Medicine Reports. 2 (3): 142–151. doi:10.1007/s40675-016-0050-3. PMC 5300077. PMID 28191449.

Ong JC, Smith CE (June 2017). "Using Mindfulness for the Treatment of Insomnia". Current Sleep Medicine Reports. 3 (2): 57–65. doi:10.1007/s40675-017-0068-1. PMC 6171769. PMID 30294523.

Kurth F, Cherbuin N, Luders E (2017). "Aging Mindfully to Minimize Cognitive Decline". Journal of Cognitive Enhancement. 1 (2): 108–14. doi:10.1007/s41465-017-0027-2. S2CID 148812598.

Xu J (November 2018). "A Tripartite Function of Mindfulness in Adjustment to Aging: Acceptance, Integration, and Transcendence". The Gerontologist. 58 (6): 1009–1015. doi:10.1093/geront/gnx100. PMID 30395235. S2CID 53218725.

Acevedo BP, Pospos S, Lavretsky H (2016). "The Neural Mechanisms of Meditative Practices: Novel Approaches for Healthy Aging". Current Behavioral Neuroscience Reports. 3 (4): 328–339. doi:10.1007/s40473-016-0098-x. PMC 5110576. PMID 27909646.

Hutton J (September 2016). "How can mindfulness help patients with skin conditions". Dermatological Nursing. 15 (3): 32–35. OCLC 6841989774.

Isgut M, Smith AK, Reimann ES, Kucuk O, Ryan J (December 2017). "The impact of psychological distress during pregnancy on the developing fetus: biological mechanisms and the potential benefits of mindfulness interventions". Journal of Perinatal Medicine. 45 (9): 999–1011. doi:10.1515/jpm-2016-0189. PMID 28141546.

Dhillon A, Sparkes E, Duarte RV (2017). "Mindfulness-Based Interventions During Pregnancy: a Systematic Review and Meta-analysis". Mindfulness. 8 (6): 1421–1437. doi:10.1007/s12671-017-0726-x. PMC 5693962. PMID 29201244.

Matvienko-Sikar K, Lee L, Murphy G, Murphy L (December 2016). "The effects of mindfulness interventions on prenatal well-being: A systematic review". Psychology & Health. 31 (12): 1415–1434. doi:10.1080/08870446.2016.1220557. PMID 27539908. S2CID 30061019.

Zeidan F, Vago DR (June 2016). "Mindfulness meditation-based pain relief: a mechanistic account". Annals of the New York Academy of Sciences. 1373 (1): 114–127. Bibcode:2016NYASA1373..114Z. doi:10.1111/nyas.13153. PMC 4941786. PMID 27398643.

Zeidan F, Martucci KT, Kraft RA, Gordon NS, McHaffie JG, Coghill RC (April 2011). "Brain mechanisms supporting the modulation of pain by mindfulness meditation". The Journal of Neuroscience. 31 (14): 5540–5548. doi:10.1523/JNEUROSCI.5791-10.2011. PMC 3090218. PMID 21471390.

Shammas MA (January 2011). "Telomeres, lifestyle, cancer, and aging". Current Opinion in Clinical Nutrition and Metabolic Care. 14 (1): 28–34. doi:10.1097/MCO.0b013e32834121b1. PMC 3370421. PMID 21102320.

Li J, Shen J, Wu G, Tan Y, Sun Y, Keller E, et al. (August 2018). "Mindful exercise versus non-mindful exercise for schizophrenia: A systematic review and meta-analysis of randomized controlled trials". Complementary Therapies in Clinical Practice. 32: 17–24. doi:10.1016/j.ctcp.2018.04.003. PMID 30057047. S2CID 51865864.

Zou L, Zhang Y, Yang L, Loprinzi PD, Yeung AS, Kong J, et al. (May 2019). "Are Mindful Exercises Safe and Beneficial for Treating Chronic Lower Back Pain? A Systematic Review and Meta-Analysis of Randomized Controlled Trials". Journal of Clinical Medicine. 8 (5): 628. doi:10.3390/jcm8050628. PMC 6571780. PMID 31072005.

Hurley D (January 14, 2014). "Breathing In vs. Spacing Out". The New York Times Magazine. Retrieved 2014-04-09.

Tang YY, Posner MI (January 2013). "Special issue on mindfulness neuroscience". Social Cognitive and Affective Neuroscience. 8 (1): 1–3. doi:10.1093/scan/nss104. PMC 3541496. PMID 22956677.

Hölzel BK, Lazar SW, Gard T, Schuman-Olivier Z, Vago DR, Ott U (November 2011). "How Does Mindfulness Meditation Work? Proposing Mechanisms of Action From a Conceptual and Neural Perspective". Perspectives on Psychological Science. 6 (6): 537–559. doi:10.1177/1745691611419671. PMID 26168376. S2CID 2218023.

Crescentini C, Capurso V (2015). "Mindfulness meditation and explicit and implicit indicators of personality and self-concept changes". Frontiers in Psychology. 6: 44. doi:10.3389/fpsyg.2015.00044. PMC 4310269. PMID 25688222.

Crescentini C, Matiz A, Fabbro F (2015). "Improving personality/character traits in individuals with alcohol dependence: the influence of mindfulness-oriented meditation". Journal of Addictive Diseases. 34 (1): 75–87. doi:10.1080/10550887.2014.991657. PMID 25585050. S2CID 8250105.

Gotink RA, Meijboom R, Vernooij MW, Smits M, Hunink MG (October 2016). "8-week Mindfulness Based Stress Reduction induces brain changes similar to traditional long-term meditation practice - A systematic review". Brain and Cognition. 108: 32–41. doi:10.1016/j.bandc.2016.07.001. PMID 27429096. S2CID 205791079.

Larouche E, Hudon C, Goulet S (January 2015). "Potential benefits of mindfulness-based interventions in mild cognitive impairment and Alzheimer's disease: an interdisciplinary per-

spective". Behavioural Brain Research. 276: 199–212. doi:
10.1016/j.bbr.2014.05.058. hdl:20.500.11794/39836. PMID
24893317. S2CID 36235259.

Last N, Tufts E, Auger LE (2017). "The Effects of Meditation
on Grey Matter Atrophy and Neurodegeneration: A Systematic Review". Journal of Alzheimer's Disease. 56 (1): 275–286.
doi:10.3233/JAD-160899. PMID 27983555.

Simon R, Engström M (2015). "The default mode network as
a biomarker for monitoring the therapeutic effects of meditation". Frontiers in Psychology. 6: 776. doi:10.3389/fpsyg.201
5.00776. PMC 4460295. PMID 26106351.

Buric I, Farias M, Jong J, Mee C, Brazil IA (2017). "What Is the
Molecular Signature of Mind-Body Interventions? A Systematic Review of Gene Expression Changes Induced by Meditation
and Related Practices". Frontiers in Immunology. 8: 670. doi:1
0.3389/fimmu.2017.00670. PMC 5472657. PMID 28670311.

Sanada K, Alda Díez M, Salas Valero M, Pérez-Yus MC, Demarzo MM, Montero-Marín J, et al. (February 2017). "Effects of
mindfulness-based interventions on biomarkers in healthy and
cancer populations: a systematic review". BMC Complementary and Alternative Medicine. 17 (1): 125. doi:10.1186/s129
06-017-1638-y. PMC 5324275. PMID 28231775.

Hölzel BK, Carmody J, Vangel M, Congleton C, Yerramsetti SM, Gard T, Lazar SW (January 2011). "Mindfulness practice leads to increases in regional brain gray matter density". Psychiatry Research. 191 (1): 36–43. doi:10.1016/j.pscychresns.2010.08.006. PMC 3004979. PMID 21071182.

de Vibe M, Bjørndal A, Fattah S, Dyrdal GM, Halland E, Tanner-Smith EE (2017). "Mindfulness-based stress reduction (MBSR) for improving health, quality of life and social functioning in adults: a systematic review and meta-analysis". Campbell Systematic Reviews. 13 (1): 1–264. doi:10.4073/csr.2017.11.

Luders E, Kurth F, Mayer EA, Toga AW, Narr KL, Gaser C (2012). "The unique brain anatomy of meditation practitioners: alterations in cortical gyrification". Frontiers in Human Neuroscience. 6: 34. doi:10.3389/fnhum.2012.00034. PMC 3289949. PMID 22393318.

Mark Wheeler (March 14, 2012). "Evidence builds that meditation strengthens the brain, UCLA researchers say". UCLA Newsroom. Archived from the original on 2014-05-05.

Fjorback, L. O.; Arendt, M.; Ornbøl, E.; Fink, P.; Walach, H. (2011). "Mindfulness-based stress reduction and mindfulness-based cognitive therapy: A systematic review of randomized controlled trials". Acta Psychiatrica Scandinavica. 124

(2): 102–119. doi:10.1111/j.1600-0447.2011.01704.x. PMID 21534932. S2CID 8410167.

"Intervention Summary: Mindfulness-Based Stress Reduction (MBSR)". Substance Abuse and Mental Health Services Administration. Archived from the original on 2015-02-09. Retrieved 2015-02-08.

Xiao, Qianguo; Hu, Chunmei; Wang, Ting (November 1, 2020). "Mindfulness Practice Makes Moral People More Moral". Mindfulness. 11 (11): 2639–2650. doi:10.1007/s126 71-020-01478-4. ISSN 1868-8535. S2CID 225428262.

Baer RA, Smith GT, Hopkins J, Krietemeyer J, Toney L (March 2006). "Using self-report assessment methods to explore facets of mindfulness". Assessment. 13 (1): 27–45. doi:10.1177/107 3191105283504. PMID 16443717. S2CID 16304094.

Baer RA, Lykins EL, Peters JR (May 1, 2012). "Mindfulness and self-compassion as predictors of psychological wellbeing in long-term meditators and matched nonmeditators". The Journal of Positive Psychology. 7 (3): 230–238. doi:10.1080/1743 9760.2012.674548. S2CID 15972961.

Bergomi C, Tschacher W, Kupper Z (December 1, 2015). "Meditation Practice and Self-Reported Mindfulness: a Cross-Sectional Investigation of Meditators and Non-Meditators Using the Comprehensive Inventory of Mindfulness Experiences (CHIME)" (PDF). Mindfulness. 6 (6): 1411–1421. doi:10.1007/s12671-015-0415-6. S2CID 141621092.

Suelmann H, Brouwers A, Snippe E (December 1, 2018). "Explaining Variations in Mindfulness Levels in Daily Life". Mindfulness. 9 (6): 1895–1906. doi:10.1007/s12671-018-0932-1 . PMC 6244631. PMID 30524516.

Gotink RA, Hermans KS, Geschwind N, De Nooij R, De Groot WT, Speckens AE (December 1, 2016). "Mindfulness and mood stimulate each other in an upward spiral: a mindful walking intervention using experience sampling". Mindfulness. 7 (5): 1114–1122. doi:10.1007/s12671-016-0550-8. PMC 5010615. PMID 27642373.

Shapiro SL, Carlson LE, Astin JA, Freedman B (March 2006). "Mechanisms of mindfulness". Journal of Clinical Psychology. 62 (3): 373–386. doi:10.1002/jclp.20237. PMID 16385481.

Chan EY (2019). "Mindfulness and willingness to try insects as food: The role of disgust". Food Quality and Preference. 71: 375–383. doi:10.1016/j.foodqual.2018.08.014 . S2CID 150289273.

Chan EY, Wang Y (September 2019). "Mindfulness changes construal level: An experimental investigation". Journal of Experimental Psychology. General. 148 (9): 1656–1664. doi:10.1037/xge0000654. PMID 31355654. S2CID 198965872.

Wachs K, Cordova JV (October 2007). "Mindful relating: exploring mindfulness and emotion repertoires in intimate relationships". Journal of Marital and Family Therapy. 33 (4): 464–481. doi:10.1111/j.1752-0606.2007.00032.x. PMID 17935530.

McLean G, Lawrence M, Simpson R, Mercer SW (May 2017). "Mindfulness-based stress reduction in Parkinson's disease: a systematic review". BMC Neurology. 17 (1): 92. doi:10.1186/s12883-017-0876-4. PMC 5433018. PMID 28506263.

Lever Taylor B, Cavanagh K, Strauss C (2016). "The Effectiveness of Mindfulness-Based Interventions in the Perinatal Period: A Systematic Review and Meta-Analysis". PLOS ONE. 11 (5): e0155720. Bibcode:2016PLoSO..1155720L. doi:10.1371/journal.pone.0155720. PMC 4868288. PMID 27182732.

Grossman P (April 2008). "On measuring mindfulness in psychosomatic and psychological research". Journal of Psychosomatic Research. 64 (4): 405–408. doi:10.1016/j.jpsychores.2008.02.001. PMID 18374739.

Wallace BA (2006). The attention revolution: Unlocking the power of the focused mind. Boston: Wisdom Publications. ISBN 978-0861712762.

Chiesa A (2012). "The Difficulty of Defining Mindfulness: Current Thought and Critical Issues". Mindfulness. 4 (3): 255–68. doi:10.1007/s12671-012-0123-4. S2CID 2244732.

Safran 2014.

Bazzano 2014.

Giesler M, Veresiu E (2014). "Creating the Responsible Consumer: Moralistic Governance Regimes and Consumer Subjectivity". Journal of Consumer Research. 41 (October): 849–67. doi:10.1086/677842. S2CID 145622639.

Safran, Jeremy D., PhD. "McMindfulness." Psychology Today. n.p., 13 June 2014. Web. 2 April 2015. <https://www.psychologytoday.com/blog/straight-talk/201406/mcmindfulness>.

Bond, Michael (September 13, 2017). "Lost in meditation: Two books argue over mindfulness". New Scientist.

Joiner, Thomas (2017). Mindlessness: The Corruption of Mindfulness in a Culture of Narcissism. Oxford University Press. ISBN 978-0-19-020062-6.

Purser R (June 14, 2019). "The mindfulness conspiracy". The Guardian. Retrieved 2020-01-15.

Shonin E (August 27, 2015). Buddhist Foundations of Mindfulness (Mindfulness in Behavioral Health) (1st ed.). Springer. pp. 90–94.

Foster D (January 23, 2016). "Is mindfulness making us ill?". The Guardian. Retrieved 2016-01-23.

Shonin E, Gordon WV, Griffiths MD (2014). "Are there risks associated with using mindfulness in the treatment of psychopathology?" (PDF). Clinical Practice. 11 (4): 389–92. doi:10.2217/cpr.14.23.

Wong SY, Chan JY, Zhang D, Lee EK, Tsoi KK (2018). "The Safety of Mindfulness-Based Interventions: a Systematic Review of Randomized Controlled Trials". Mindfulness. 9 (5): 1344–1357. doi:10.1007/s12671-018-0897-0. S2CID 255783169.

www.ingramcontent.com/pod-product-compliance
Lightning Source LLC
Chambersburg PA
CBHW050328160726
48002CB00001B/222